# ARTEMIS

Virgin Goddess of the Hunt & Moon

# ARTEMIS
*Virgin Goddess of the Hunt & Moon*

## Sorita d'Este

Published by Avalonia
www.avaloniabooks.com

Published by Avalonia

BM Avalonia
London
WC1N 3XX
England, UK

WWW.AVALONIABOOKS.COM

Artemis: Virgin Goddess of the Hunt & Moon

Copyright © Sorita d'Este, 2024

ISBN: 978-1-910191-26-2
(Paperback)

First edition, August 2005
Second Edition, June 2024

Photographs by Sorita d'Este, 2015-2023

Illustrations by Brian Andrews, 2005

Designed and produced by Avalonia Ltd
BM Avalonia, London, WC1N 3XX, United Kingdom
WWW.AVALONIABOOKS.COM

All Rights Reserved.

British Library Cataloguing in Publication Data. A catalogue record for this book is available from the British Library.

Every effort has been made to credit material and obtain permission from copyright holders to use their work. If you notice any error or omission please notify the publisher so that corrections can be incorporated into future editions of this work. The information provided in this book hopes to inspire and inform. The author and publisher assume no responsibility for the effects, or lack thereof, obtained from the practices described in this book.

The reproduction of any part of this book, other than for review purposes, is strictly forbidden, in all formats, without the prior written consent of Avalonia Ltd and the copyright holders.

*For Kate.*

# GRATITUDE

My forever thanks to Kate, who inspired me to make this book happen. I miss you.

My heartfelt appreciation goes to Galatea, a steadfast friend, for your unwavering support as a guiding Priestess, embodying the very essence of devotion. Your gentle encouragement guided me to complete this second edition of *Artemis*, and to continue my work on my forthcoming *Divine Diana*.

With thanks to my friends Christina Moraiti and Kay Gillard for helping with the proofreading and final edits. I am blessed to have you both in my life.

And finally, to my nonna Santuzza Gonzaga who first introduced me to the classics as a child, including the poetry of Edmund Clarence Stedman (1833-1908) where I first remember hearing her name:

> *Of Artemis,—her bow, with points drawn back,*
> *A golden hue on her white rounded breast*
> *Reflecting, while the arrow's ample barb*
> *Gleams o'er her hand, and at his heart is aim'd.*

# PREFACE

It is such a privilege to write this introduction to this new edition of my book Artemis on the island of Ortygia in Sicily. Here tourists continue to learn about the stories of the gods every day as they stare at the fresh waters of the Arethousa Spring, or gaze in wonder at the incredible fountain depicting the myth of the nymph protected by the Goddess from the unwanted advances of the river god.

When I compiled the first edition of this book, way back in 2005, I did so out of a desire to open up discussion and understanding about the huntress. Artemis is one of the most enduring goddesses of the ancient world and perhaps the most widely worshipped of all the Greek goddesses. She was Potnia Theron, the Lady of the Wild Animals, and due to Greek – and later Roman – practice of *interpretatio* (translating and equating local deities to one of their own) Artemis subsumed into her worship qualities of many other goddesses and would herself later be correlated to the Roman *Diana*.

It is impossible to know what this book would have looked like if I was writing it now, and I have tried my best to not rewrite it completely for this second edition – instead simply updating and correcting some things along the way.

When I first wrote it, I was deeply involved in the practice of *Initiatory Craft* or Wicca, and it was within that tradition that one of my teachers encouraged me to consider Artemis as a goddess not only of the Moon, but also of the Sun – due to the metal and colour gold and also saffron being associated with her so much. The most significant change I have made to this book is to change the subtitle away from "Goddess of the *Sun & Moon*" as it was in the original edition to Goddess of the *Hunt & Moon*. I feel it was a mistake to highlight the possible connection to the Sun so much all that time ago – and it has been bothering me all these years! Artemis does arguably have some solar attributes, but her association with the Moon is definitely dominant.

I hope that you will find value in the work I gathered here, and that you will find this second edition to be an improvement and more enjoyable read.

*xx Sorita d'Este*

Ortygia, Sicily, 2023

# TABLE OF CONTENTS

1. WHO WAS ARTEMIS? ........................................ 15
2. THE BIRTH OF THE DIVINE TWINS ................. 25
3. TEMPLES & SANCTUARIES OF ARTEMIS ......... 33
4. FESTIVALS OF ARTEMIS .................................. 50
5. MYTHS & LEGENDS ......................................... 56
6. TITLES OF ARTEMIS ........................................ 64
7. A VIRGIN GODDESS ........................................ 92
8. GODDESS OF WOMEN ..................................... 98
9. LADY OF THE HUNT & WILD ANIMALS ........ 101
10. GODDESS OF THE DANCE & SONG .............. 117
11. GODDESS OF WATER .................................... 123
12. WARRIOR GODDESS ...................................... 125
13. THE REVENGE OF ARTEMIS .......................... 127
14. THE BRIGHT SHINING MOON ...................... 132
15. DIVINE RELATIONSHIPS ................................ 136
17. THE COMPANIONS OF ARTEMIS .................. 149
18. TEMPLE ATTENDANTS .................................. 157
19. ARTEMIS & MEN ........................................... 160
20. ARTEMIS' SYMBOLS ...................................... 162

BIBLIOGRAPHY ..................................................... 166

INDEX .................................................................. 171

FIGURE 1 - ARTEMIS THE HUNTER, DRAWING BY BRIAN ANDREWS BASED ON THE STATUE IN THE LOUVRE MUSEUM, PARIS.

# INTRODUCTION

Artemis, the ancient Greek Virgin Goddess of the hunt and moon, has captured the imagination of many people throughout the ages. Poets have written about Artemis as the ultimate unobtainable prize, and artists have portrayed her as surrounded by her hunting dogs, wild animals, and, of course, with her bow and quiver of arrows, always ready for the kill. For thousands of years, pilgrims have visited her temples and sanctuaries to ask for her help with childbirth, healing and devotion, and today, those of us interested in history and the gods of our ancestors still marvel at the marvel that was the Temple of Artemis of Ephesus, one of the seven wonders of the ancient world.

This book is the result of research and work I started in 2000 when I started a research project on the goddess Hekate with an intense and fevered passion. My research took me down various avenues, and time after time, Artemis (and the goddess Diana) waited, in one form or another, at the end of them. My work with Hekate has since then resulted in two anthologies: *Hekate: Keys to the Crossroads* (2006) and *Hekate: Her Sacred Fires* (2010), as well as *Hekate: Liminal Rites* (2009, with David Rankine) and the *Circle for Hekate project* (since 2017).

When this book was first written, there were no accessible books exclusively dedicated to the history, stories, myths and powers of the goddess Artemis. This felt wrong – Artemis was one of the most enduring goddesses of the ancient world, whose worship adapted and changed through the centuries and in the 21st century, she continues to receive homage – both in art and culture and in the household worship of many who are drawn back to the old religions in a world where monotheism is no longer seen as the only way to be. This book is now in its second edition and is one of many exploring this fascinating goddess.

When I compiled the information in this book, I aimed to provide an overview of Artemis – a starting point that I hoped others would take, add to and evolve. The worship of Artemis was nearly universal, and additionally, it became conflated with that of Hekate and Diana, as well as Selene and many other goddesses along the way. So much so that it is sometimes nearly impossible to know where the one stops and the other starts! At times, some of the stories will appear to overlap or be contrary; this is inevitable considering the long period of worship and the broad geographical region in which Artemis received worship. As with the stories of the other gods, local influences and the flux in popularity of different cults over time will change and evolve both ritual practices and mythologies.

Artemis is so much more than the Virgin Huntress or Moon Goddess, the simplistic image promoted over the last century. She is a mysterious, complex goddess who fiercely protects those she cares for. Artemis is a lunar goddess, a virgin presiding over childbirth, worshipped by warriors and by young girls for the protection of their virginity. She is vengeful and capable of sending disease with her arrows, but she is also a goddess of ecstatic song and dance. She is a huntress and the mountain dwelling goddess who protects the wild and animals.

Artemis is many things, but if you look upon the face of the young and innocent huntress in her short tunic - whatever you do, and whoever you are - don't ever make the mistake of underestimating or disrespecting her!

*Hear me, Jove's daughter, celebrated queen,*
*Bacchian and Titan, of a noble mien:*
*In darts rejoicing and on all to shine,*
*Torch-bearing Goddess, Dictynna divine;*
*O'er births presiding, and thyself a maid,*
*To labour-pangs imparting ready aid:*
*Dissolver of the zone and wrinkl'd care,*
*Fierce huntress, glorying in the Sylvan war:*
*Swift in the course, in dreadful arrows skill'd,*
*Wandering by night, rejoicing in the field:*
*Of manly form, erect, of bounteous mind,*
*Illustrious dæmon, nurse of human kind:*
*Immortal, earthly, bane of monsters fell,*
*'Tis thine, blest maid, on woody hills to dwell:*
*Foe of the stag, whom woods and dogs delight,*
*In endless youth who flourish fair and bright.*
*O, universal queen, august, divine,*
*A various form, Cydonian pow'r, is thine:*
*Dread guardian Goddess, with benignant mind*
*Auspicious, come to Mystic rites inclin'd;*
*Give earth a store of beauteous fruits to bear,*
*Send gentle Peace, and Health with lovely hair,*
*And to the mountains drive Disease and Care.*

*Orphic Hymn, circa 2<sup>nd</sup> century CE,*
*Translated by Thomas Taylor, 18th century*

*Muse, sing of Artemis, sister of the Far-shooter,
the virgin who delights in arrows,
who was fostered with Apollo.
She waters her horses from Meles deep in reeds, and
swiftly drives her all-golden chariot through Smyrna to
vine-clad Claros where Apollo,
god of the silver bow,*

*sits waiting for the far-shooting goddess
who delights in arrows.
And so hail to you,
Artemis, in my song and to all goddesses as well.
Of you first I sing and with you I begin;
now that I have begun with you,
I will turn to another song.*

Homeric Hymn to Artemis, Homer – translated by Evelyn-White

# 1.
# WHO WAS ARTEMIS?

To those who worshipped in her temples and sanctuaries in ancient times, Artemis was a goddess of childbirth and initiation rites for young girls. To them, she was a gentle goddess fiercely protective of those she cared for, especially her mother and virgin attendants. She was an unparalleled huntress at home with wild animals in the wilderness and mountains. She played a significant role in many of the myths of the Ancient Greek world, held an esteemed position as one of the Olympian Gods in their religious life and much more. Her temple at Ephesus earned its place as one of the Seven Wonders of the Ancient World,[1] a testament to the immense popularity and importance Artemis had.

## FAMILY

The twin sister of the solar god Apollo, Artemis was, according to Hesiod, the daughter of the Titan goddess Leto and the king of the Olympian gods, Zeus. Leto's parents were Coeus and Phoebe. Coeus was one of the older Titans and was one of the poles or pillars that kept the heavens and earth apart; he may have been an oracular god. Phoebe was a goddess of bright intellect and light, and she was the third deity to preside over the Oracle of Delphi, which in turn passed to her grandchild Apollo. Coeus and Phoebe also give birth to Asteria, who is the mother of Hekate. Both Asteria and Hekate are linked to divination and oracles.

Zeus' parents were Rhea and Kronos. Rhea was the Mother of the Gods, a fertility goddess whose name might mean *flow*. Kronos was the King of the Titans and the God of Time. They are also the parents of Poseidon, Hades, Hera, Demeter and many more. Coeus, Phoebe, Rhea and Kronos were all the children of Gaia (Earth) and Ouranos (Starry Heavens), the grandparents of Artemis and Apollo.

---

[1] Alongside the Great Pyramid of Giza, The Hanging Gardens of Babylon, The Colossus of Rhodes, The Statue of Zeus at Olympia, The Mausoleum at Halicarnassus and the Lighthouse of Alexandria.

While this is the best known and accepted parentage she is given, some writers claimed that she was the daughter of Demeter (rather than Leto), or according to Herod II, her parents were Dionysus and Isis, with Leto being her nursemaid. Similarly, some accounts hold that Artemis and Apollo were siblings rather than twins. In these accounts, Artemis is born first, assisting with the birth of Apollo, and their parents remain Leto and Zeus.

# ORIGINS

The cult of the goddess Artemis has ancient origins dating back to prehistoric times in Anatolia, present-day Türkiye, and perhaps further East and South. We don't know what names earlier tribes used for her, but we can recognise her through images and the symbols used in many ancient images of a Mother Goddess who was worshipped throughout Asia Minor. In this, her history is intricately linked to that of Hekate, Rhea, Kybele, Selene and later also that of the Roman Diana – all of whom share their origins in the spiritual beliefs and practices of the same region and the cult of the Mother Goddess.

There is evidence for her worship during the Mycenaean period (circa 1600–1100 BCE), with her worship peaking during the Archaic and Classical periods (800–323 BCE), continuing into the Hellenistic and Roman periods. The Mycenaeans were known for their advanced culture, military prowess, advanced engineering and sophisticated architecture. They built several impressive citadels, including the Citadel of Mycenae, associated with the legendary king Agamemnon. Their civilization is linked to the stories of Greek mythology, particularly the Trojan War and the epic poems of Homer, the Iliad, and the Odyssey. They produced the earliest known forms of Greek writing, *Linear A & B*, through which we know a little about their culture and beliefs. However, their culture suddenly declined by the end of the 12th century BCE, and almost all their power centres were destroyed or abandoned. There is a lot of debate about what caused this sudden decline, and scholars and archaeologists have not satisfactorily agreed upon a reason.

The goddess Artemis is likely the culmination of the coming together of many different goddesses over the course of millennia.

Influences from around the Aegean, Mediterranean, Asia Minor and the Middle East can all be found in her stories and depictions, as can be expected from a goddess who enjoyed tremendous popularity. At some ancient temples, we can find evidence linking Greece with Anatolia, Syria, Mesopotamia and Egypt – and undoubtedly further afield. She is closely associated with the Lady of the Animals, *Potnia Theron*, depicted throughout the abovementioned regions. In these depictions, Artemis is depicted as standing, often winged, with different animals by her side – most frequently lions, leopards, deer, dogs, swans, geese and other birds.

Temples and sanctuaries to Artemis existed throughout the Greek world and stretched into Anatolia[2] and Greek colonies as far afield as Sicily and Gaul[3].

## MEANING OF HER NAME

The exact meaning of the name Artemis is not known for certain, not even in the ancient world. Two of the best-known explanations came from Strabo and Plato.

The Roman writer Strabo suggested a meaning for it in his writings, saying that Artemis made people *Artemeas*, which means something like *safe and sound*.[4]

Plato suggested that Artemis took her name from her healthy (*artemes*) and well-ordered nature and possibly due to her disliking sexual intercourse (*ton aroton misesasa*).[5]

## PHYSICAL DESCRIPTIONS

There are two distinct primary types of depictions of the goddess named Artemis: The Ephesian Artemis and the Huntress.

The likely reason for this is that the name *Artemis* was applied to an earlier goddess worshipped on or in the region of Ephesus, just like the Romans would later refer to the deity worshipped at the

---

2 Asia Minor, modern Türkiye.
3 Modern day France.
4 Strabo 14.1.6.
5 Plato, Cratylus.

site by their name of Diana. This process of interpretation or translation allows the newly arrived invaders (in this case, Greek or Roman) to interpret the local culture and their religions based on their knowledge and gods. When there are significant similarities, they may translate the names of the gods into the names of their similar deities.

The Winged Goddess     The Ephesian Goddess     The Huntress

*(Illustrations by Brian Andrews, 2005)*

Artemis is also depicted as Potnia Theron, Lady of the Animals. This form may have been the older form of Artemis, the Mountain Mother or Great Mother Goddess.

The three most prominent depictions of Artemis are (from left to right) the Winged Goddess (as Potnia Theron), the Ephesian Goddess and the Huntress.

## THE WINGED GODDESS

Many earlier representations of Artemis show her as a winged goddess. Examples include the image of the Francois Vase and a gold necklace found on the island of Rhodes. In both these images, the goddess is *Potnia Theron*, the Lady of the Beasts. In this depiction, she holds a large feline on the vase in her right hand and a stag on the other side.

The necklace shows her holding two large felines, which could be either lions or leopards. Winged depictions of goddesses are unusual amongst the Greek gods, although not unique - the goddesses Nike (goddess of victory) and Nemesis (goddess of vengeance) are both also depicted as winged.

See Chapter 9: Lady of the Hunt & Wild Animals for more about Artemis' connection with wild animals and Potnia Theron, Lady of the Animals.

# THE EPHESIAN GODDESS

The depiction of Artemis, famously associated with Ephesus, is one of the most unusual and memorable. The original icon does not survive, but replicas from antiquity show the goddess standing upright, adorned with the images of many wild animals on both her body and headdress. The headdress worn by the Ephesian goddess includes a turret crown, often depicting recognizable city features, suggesting her status as the city's primary deity and protective role.

It also shows Artemis with numerous oval protrusions on her chest. Later Christian writers interpreted these as female breasts, but there is no evidence to support this theory. Nontheless, it was popularised by the famous fountain in the gardens of the Villa d'Este in Tivoli, Italy. Here, a 15th century sculptor, taking inspiration from a Roman copy of the Ephesian Goddess now held in the Archaeological Museum of Naples, creatively transformed the protrusions into breasts from which water pours. The garden of Villa d'Este is amongst the most famous and influential to emerge from the Renaissance, and many other European gardens took their inspiration from it – and even today, *The Mother Nature Fountain* (depicting the Ephesian Goddess with breasts) is one of the most popular and recognisable features of these extensive gardens.

The carvings on these statues are detailed, showing all kinds of symbols and animals. The oval protrusions do not have nipples or other features suggestive of a female breast. Other suggestions are that they are bull's testicles, a beaded necklace, a warrior breastplate, eggs, beehives or bee cells (from which the larvae hatch). The hypothesis that the protrusions are linked to bees holds appeal, given the close association of bees with the Ephesian Artemis. The Ephesian Goddess' priestesses were known as Melissae (bees), and images of bees were featured on her iconic statues and the city's coins.

Also, see Chapter 3: Temples & Sanctuaries; Artemis of Ephesus for further information.

## THE HUNTRESS

> *"Sosis, Phila and Polycrates dedicate this harp, this bow and these intricate nets. The archer dedicates his bow of horn, the musician her tortoise-shell lyre and the hunter his woven nets. Let the first win prize for archery, the next for harp-playing and the third in the hunting world."*[6]

Artemis was most often portrayed as the huntress with her bow and quiver of arrows, which had been given to her as a young girl by the Cyclops, the one-eyed giants who specialized in making weapons, at the behest of Zeus. In these depictions, she is typically shown with her hair tied back or otherwise fastened.

Artemis was also sometimes shown carrying hunting spears, emphasising her role as a huntress.

> *"Tired after the hunt, the goddess loved her Nymphs to bathe her with the water's balm ... she gave her spear and quiver and bow unstrung to an attendant Nymph."*[7]

The most popular modern portrayals of Artemis are based on images such as the sculpture known as *Artemis of Versailles*, which is currently on display in the Louvre, Paris. This is one of many Roman statues which are believed to be copies of an earlier Greek depiction of the goddess. Artemis is shown with her quiver of arrows, usually in a running position with a stag, deer or dog at her side, reaching for an arrow in her quiver.

This image of Artemis as the hunter inspired later artists, including Renoir. It is also the image widely used for the Roman Diana.

## BEAUTY & HEIGHT

Artemis was always described as being very tall and beautiful, overshadowing her companion nymphs. She was frequently depicted with animal companions, as would be expected for a

---

6 Antipater, The Offering of the Winners.
7 Metamorphoses 3.138.

hunting goddess and mistress of the animals. This is supported by Homer in the Odyssey, when he comments that even amongst the most beautiful maidens, Artemis was conspicuous:

*"With head and forehead Artemis overtops the rest (of her companion Nymphs), and though all are lovely, there is no mistaking which is she."*[8]

Artemis is also described in the Iliad, where her beauty and height are both emphasised[9], and Euripides described Artemis as the *"fairest of all that are"*.[10]

Ovid described her in his Metamorphoses, saying that she stood a head taller than her attendant nymphs.[11]

*"At once, seeing a man, all naked as they were, the Nymphae, beating their breasts, filled the whole grove with sudden screams and clustered round Artemis to clothe her body with their own. But she stood taller, a head taller than them all.."* [12]

The Titan goddess Aura, when she was a companion to Artemis, commented[13] on the roundness of Artemis' breasts and her soft arms and said that with her beauty and figure, Artemis could also be a goddess of marriage.

In Sophocles' Oedipus the King, Artemis is described as having golden-snooded hair.[14] Gold is also emphasised in regard to her snood a headband worn by unmarried women.

## CONTRADICTIONS?

It is not difficult to see why the different images of Artemis - winged, Ephesian and Huntress - would be considered as being contrary and maybe even different goddesses. Each of these images is probably the result of the conflation of two or more goddesses,

---

8 Odyssey 6.102.
9 Iliad 6.93.109.
10 Euripides, Hippolytus.
11 Ovid, Metamorphoses 3.138.
12 Ovid, Metamorphoses 3.138.
13 Nonnus, Dionysiaca 48.360.
14 Sophocles, Oedipus the King, 211.

cultures or other ideas, and they all represent the goddess Artemis during the Hellenistic and later Roman periods. At Ephesus, the goddess represented the Magna Mater, the Great Mother – it is possible that locals perhaps also recognised another local goddess in the image and its symbolism, at least for a few generations. It is likely that these goddesses were worshipped together in an earlier cult in the same and nearby regions and became conflated.

For the Ephesians, Artemis was Artemis, no matter how she was depicted. They used different images alongside each other, as illustrated by this coin, an Ephesian stater dated to the 2nd century. It shows Artemis as the huntress with her bow and quiver on the one side and Artemis as the Ephesian goddess on the obverse (right). Alongside the Ephesian goddess is depicted a stag and bee (by her feet) and a star (by her head) – all important symbols associated with Artemis.

*Figure 2 - Ephesos, Ionia, 133 - 88 BCE.*

# DATELINE FOR SOURCE MATERIAL

Homer - 9th-8th century BCE
Hesiod - 8th-7th century BCE
The Homeric Hymns - 8th-4th century BCE
Alkman – 7th century BCE
Greek Lyric Fragments - 7th-6th century BCE
Etymologicum Magnum – 7th-6th century BCE
Hipponax – 6th century BCE
Aiskhylos – 6th-5th century BCE
Euripides – 5th century BCE
Herodotus - 5th century BCE
Pindar - 5th century BCE
Sophocles – 5th century BCE
Aristophanes - 5th-4th century BCE
Plato – 5th-4th century BCE
Xenophon – 5th-4th century BCE
The Orphic Hymns - uncertain century BCE
Antipater – 4th century BCE
Theocritus – 4th-3rd century BCE
Callimachus – 3rd century BCE
Apollonius Rhodius - 3rd century BCE
Apollodorus - 2nd century BCE
Servius Sulpicius Rufus – 2nd century BCE
Cicero – 1st century BCE
Diodorus Siculus - 1st century BCE
Virgil - 1st century BCE
Homerica, The Contest of Homer & Hesiod, Aethiopica, Cypria - BCE
Ovid - 1st century BCE - 1st century CE
Strabo - 1st century BCE - 1st century CE
Pliny the Elder - 1st century CE
Statius - 1st century CE
Valerius Flaccus – 1st century CE

Plutarch - 1st-2nd century CE
Ptolemy Hephaestion - 1st-2nd century CE
Antoninus Liberalis – 2nd century CE
Apuleius – 2nd century CE
Hyginus - 2nd century CE
Pausanias - 2nd century CE
Philostratus - 2nd century CE
Aelian - 2nd-3rd century CE
Cassius Dio – 2nd-3rd century CE
Oppian – 2nd-3rd century CE
Athenaios – 3rd century CE
Lactantius – 3rd-4th century CE
Porphyry – 3rd-4th century CE
Quintus Smyrnaeus - 4th century CE
Nonnus - 5th century CE
Proclus – 5th century CE
Colluthus - 5th-6th century CE
Suidas - 10th century CE

# 2.
# THE BIRTH OF THE DIVINE TWINS

> *"And Leto was joined in love with*
> *Zeus who holds the aegis,*
> *and bare Apollo and Artemis delighting in arrows,*
> *children lovely above all the sons of Heaven."*
> The Theogony, by Hesiod, trans. Evelyn-White

Artemis was the older twin sister of the god Apollo. They were born of a union between the Titan goddess Leto and the Olympian Zeus, king of the gods, Zeus, well-known for his many amorous conquests. Zeus was married to the goddess Hera, the goddess of marriage and was frequently involved in myths and stories that revolved around her attempts to punish Zeus' lovers and their offspring.

In Pausanias, an alternative parentage is given for Artemis, suggesting that her mother is the earth goddess Demeter rather than Leto.

> *"That Artemis was the daughter, not of Leto but of Demeter, which is the Egyptian account, the Greeks learned from Aiskhylos the son of Euphorion."*[15]

However, as the most frequently given accounts name Zeus and Leto as her parents, that is what I will focus on here.

Classical writers gave varying accounts of the story of Leto's pregnancy and birth, each placing a different emphasis on various parts of the story. Many texts, including the writings of Apollodorus, Ovid, Pausanias, Strabo, the Dionysiaca, the Greek Lyric V Scolia Frag 886, Hesiod's Theogony, the Homeric Hymns and Pindar's Processional Song on Delos all gave varying accounts of the events that follow.

---

[15] Pausanias 8.37.3.

# LETO'S PREGNANCY, EXILE & THE BIRTH OF THE TWINS

Hera, wife to Zeus, was furious when she discovered that Leto was pregnant with her husband. She sent the Python of Delphi (a serpent, or a dragon in some versions) to chase Leto across the land, pursuing her and preventing her from stopping or resting anywhere to give birth. Hera also forced the rulers of all the various lands to deny Leto sanctuary, preventing her from giving birth on land. At one point, Leto, desperate for sanctuary, shapeshifted and took on the form of a wolf so she could hide with a pack of wolves.

Figure 3 - Title: Latona and Her Sleeping Twins, Apollo And Diana/Artemis By Francesco Antonio Meloni (Italian, Bologna 1676–1713 Vienna)

Leto travelled through many different places while constantly being chased by the Python. Several of these locations would later be named in honour of the twins and their auspicious birth.

The geographer Pausanias mentioned Zoster in Attica, home of a shrine to Leto, Artemis and Apollo. It was at Zoster that Leto let loose her girdle and managed to get some rest before continuing her journey to find a safe place to give birth to her children. The term *zoster* originates from the Greek word for girdle or belt.

## THE PEOPLE OF KOS

Herodas named the island of Kos as Leto's place of birth, and perhaps this explains why, as Callimachus wrote, the people of Kos were the first to offer Leto a place to rest and birth her children. However, when the unborn Apollo heard this, he spoke to his mother from her womb, declaring that Kos had a different destiny. Kos later became associated with the son of Apollo, the God Asclepius, and an important healing temple. During the Hellenistic period, it was home to a medical school.

## ZEUS & THE NORTH WIND

According to writers such as Callimachus and Pseudo-Hyginus, Zeus stepped in to lend a helping hand at the last minute. He commanded the North Wind Boreas to bear Leto safely away from the Python to safety on the island of Ortygia with the help of Poseidon. It was here that Leto could finally rest and complete her labour.

## THE BIRTHPLACE OF THE TWINS: ORTYGIA

Apollo speaking to his mother and prophesying the future destiny of Kos also sets him on his course as a future God of Oracles. Apolo then goes on to instruct his mother on where she should go instead:

> *"But mark thou, mother: there is to be seen in the water a tiny island, wandering over the seas. Her feet abide not in one place, but on the tide she swims even as stalks of asphodel, where the South wind or the East wind blows, whithersoever the sea carried her. Thither do thou carry me. For she shall welcome thy coming. When he had spoken thus much, the other islands in the sea ran away. But thou, Asteria, lover of song, didst come down from Euboea to visit the round*

*Cyclades – not long ago, but still behind thee trailed
the sea-weed of Geraestus ..., seeing the unhappy lady
in the grievous pangs of birth: 'Hera, do to me what
thou wilt. For I heed not their threats. Cross, crossover,
Leto, unto me.' "*[16]

Ortygia means quail. Three places claim to be the Ortygia where Leto birthed the sacred twins:

- Ortygia, a Greek Island now known as Delos;
- Ortygia, Sicily, a small island which is part of the city of Syracuse in Italy;
- Ortygia, a location near the ruins of the temple of the Ephesian Artemis, just outside Selcuk in Türkiye today.

Ortygia came into being when the star goddess Asteria, escaping the sexual embrace of Zeus, threw herself into the ocean, becoming a floating island. For this reason, it is sometimes known by the name Asteria, which may have been its earlier name. Asteria was the sister of Leto and the mother of the goddess Hekate (by Perses). Before birthing Hekate,[17] she was pursued by the god Zeus, who had set his sights on her. By shapeshifting, she escaped his embrace, eventually – in the form of a quail – throwing herself into the ocean.

Because of Ortygia's origin story, it was described as a floating island unattached to the ocean floor. Again, this may provide another reason why Leto was able to give birth there. Hera forbade Leto from giving birth on solid earth, so a floating island would have provided a loophole. Callimachus wrote about it, saying:

*"But no constraint afflicted thee, but free upon the open
sea thou didst float; and thy name of old was Asteria,
since like a star thou didst leap from heaven into the
deep moat, fleeing wedlock with Zeus. Until then,
golden Leto consorted not with thee: then thou wert still
Asteria and wert not yet called Delos. Oft-times did
sailors coming from the town of fair-haired Troezen*

---

16 Callimachus, Hymn 4 to Delos, Trans Mair, 1921
17 Like Artemis, Hekate is linked to Eileithyia the birth goddess who attended the infant Zeus after Rhea gave birth to him on the island of Crete.

*unto Ephyra within the Saronic gulf descry thee, and on their way back from Ephyra saw thee no more there, but thou hadst run to the swift straits of the narrow Euripus with its sounding stream. And the same day, turning thy back on the waters of the sea of Chalcis, thou didst swim to the Sunian headland of the Athenians or to Chios or to the wave-washed breast of the Maiden's Isle, not yet called Samos – where the nymphs of Mycalessos, neighbours of Ancaeus, entertained thee..."*

## DELOS, GREEK ISLAND

Today Delos is a UNESCO world heritage site, and one of the primary reasons cited for this is that the island is the birthplace of Apollo and Artemis. While the other two Ortygias also lay claim to being their birthplace, Delos has long been the most popular candidate.

Occupied since at least 3000 BCE, the sanctuary to Apollo on Delos dates to around 900 BCE. Callimachus described it in the 3rd century BCE[18] as "the most sacred island", and after the declaration for the island to become a free port (no taxes payable) in 167 BCE, the island became one of the world's wealthiest and greatest commercial centres. Ironically, its wealth may have contributed to its downfall; after being twice looted in the 1st century BCE, it started falling into disrepair. Subsequent cultures settled there, looting the remains. During the Ottoman occupation burnt the columns of many temples to manufacture lime.

Notwithstanding, the entire island remains covered in archaeological remains related to Artemis, Apollo and the gods associated with them.

The practice of sacred begging in the names of Opis and Arge was said to be practised here by women, following an ancient tradition linked to the Mother Goddess. Herodotus wrote that Olen of Lycia wrote the hymn used by the begging women on Delos.

---

18 Callimachus, Hymn 4 to Delos.

FIGURE 3 - FOUNTAIN OF DIANA, ORTIGIA, SYRACUSE. THIS FOUNTAIN SHOWS THE GODDESS WITH THE NYMPH ARETHOUSA AND THE RIVER GOD. THE GODDESS AS DIANA ENJOYED CONTINUED POPULARITY DURING THE ROMAN PERIOD, BOTH IN WHAT IS NOW ITALY AND BEYOND.

## ORTYGIA, SYRACUSE (SICILY, ITALY)

This Ortygia is a small islet off the coast of Sicily and part of Syracuse. This city has a rich and ancient history, as is attested by the many archaeological remains found here, which include the remains of a temple to Demeter. On the island, you can still visit the remains of temples to Apollo, Artemis and Athena. The Doric temple of Athena was repurposed over the centuries - becoming a church, then a mosque and is now the Duomo (Cathedral) of Syracuse. Because of how it was repurposed, the temple is very well preserved today.

The temple of Apollo has been excavated in part and can be viewed from the street level today. Christians repurposed the Artemision, and after falling into disuse, other buildings were erected on top of its ruins. Thanks to some ingenious modern engineering, the site has been excavated and can be visited under the buildings now standing on the site.

This Ortygia is also home to a remarkable and powerful freshwater spring that flows just meters away from the ocean and is, according to legend, the spring is the nymph Arethousa, who was turned into the spring to save her from the unwanted advances of a river god. See *Artemis & Fish*.

## ORTYGIA, EPHESUS

This Ortygia is a small grove near the Temple of Artemis of Ephesus, which the Ephesians claimed as the birthplace of the twins.

## EILEITHYIA: GODDESS OF CHILDBIRTH

In the version of the story recounted in the Homeric Hymns, Eileithyia, a goddess of childbirth, was kept occupied on Mount Olympus by Hera to stop her from attending the birth. However, the other goddesses sent the messenger goddess Iris to fetch Eileithyia and take her to Leto, which she did.

Although the birth of Artemis had been straightforward, that of Apollo was not, and he did not leave his mother's womb until Eileithyia arrived. Sometimes, Artemis assists with the birth of her twin brother – even though she was only a newborn herself! Of course, the rules for the gods are always different.

Eileithyia as an epithet is used for the goddesses Hera, Hekate and Artemis, identifying them as goddesses of birth. Eileithyia can be translated as *she who comes to help* or *relieve* and was depicted as a woman bearing a torch. She can be compared to Lucina (*light*) and Natio (*birth*) in the later Roman pantheon. There were also multiple Eileithyae who were said to be the daughters of the goddess Hera.

Callimachus wrote that the messenger goddess Iris informed Hera about Leto's labour on Ortygia. Initially furious with Leto, Hera places a curse on all those impregnated by Zeus, wishing them worse birthing conditions than those of underprivileged mill women. However, Hera's anger subsides after learning that Asteria (as Ortygia) is sheltering Leto and knowing she successfully resisted Zeus' advances.

> *"But against Asteria am I no wise angered for this sin, nor can I do to her so unkindly as I should – for very wrongly has she done a favour to Leto. Howbeit I honour her exceedingly for that she did not desecrate my bed, but instead of Zeus preferred the sea."*[19]

On Ortygia, Leto gives birth to the twins, forging a profound bond between the sisters. As a reward for her pivotal role, Asteria is awarded adamantine pillars, securing her to the ocean floor. The island is renamed Delos, becoming a significant religious pilgrimage destination for many centuries.

In alternative versions of this myth, Zeus changed Leto into a quail to help her reach Delos.

## BIRTHDAY CELEBRATIONS

In honour of the birth of Artemis and Apollo, the festival of First Fruits or Thargelia was celebrated in the month of Thargelion, corresponding to our modern May or June. It is celebrated over two days to mark Artemis' birth on the 6th and Apollo's on the 7th. It is likely that the first day of the Thargelia was a day of purification and driving things out, during which scapegoating rituals were sometimes used. The 7th day was dedicated to bringing new things in and on which offerings and devotion were offered to the Gods.

In some places, the 6th day of every month was considered sacred to Artemis and the 7th to her brother Apollo.

---

19 Callimachus, Hymn 4 to Delos, Trans Mair, 1921

# 3.
# TEMPLES & SANCTUARIES OF ARTEMIS

Her devotees constructed temples and sanctuaries in veneration of the goddess Artemis throughout the ancient Greek world. These places of worship focussed on Artemis were not static, and although many ritual practices often remained the same for centuries, they were not static and did change with the times. These sacred sites stood as tangible expressions of devotion and served as focal points for religious ceremonies and a testament to the popularity of her cult.

Pausanias, in his classic work *Guide to Greece*, a 2nd century CE travel guide to the Greek world, listed many temples and shrines of Artemis. Evidence for the location of Artemis' temples can also be found through an examination of her epithets, many of which refer to the sites she was associated with. See *Chapter 6, Titles of Artemis*. Pausanias' work and location-specific epithets, combined with archaeological evidence and places named and described in surviving plays, comedies, poetry and other literary works, provide us with many insights into Artemis' sacred sites.

Temples were often built with a focus on a statue of the deity. Based on accounts of devotional rites to Artemis, we know that many were held around statues, and legends illustrate the great importance placed upon specific cult statues, which were used in ceremonies.

An unusual example of the use of a statue can be found in the accounts of rites held at Sparta to Artemis Orthia. Young men were ritually scourged here while a priestess bearing the wooden cult statue of Artemis looked on. In another early account, young girls and boys carried a statue of Artemis Ephesia out to a field near the sea, where they danced and sang around it.[20]

---

[20] Etymologicum Magnum.

Communities often constructed Artemis' temples and sanctuaries near springs or rivers, driven by practical and spiritual considerations. Devotees frequently made offerings into the water to petition or offer gratitude to the goddess at these places.

The best-known of Artemis' temples are those at Ephesus and Brauron.

## ARTEMIS OF EPHESUS

The temple of Artemis at Ephesus was and remains the most famous temple to Artemis and all of the ancient goddesses. Hyginus wrote that the temple of Artemis at Ephesus was one of the Seven Wonders of the Ancient World[21], and the temple was praised and written about by people from all over the ancient world. Artemis was celebrated at this temple with the title of Artemis *Ephesia*, meaning simply *of Ephesus*. Pausanias wrote of Artemis Ephesia, writing, *"All cities worship Artemis Ephesia"*.[22] He wrote that she was universally held in very high renown due to the antiquity and size of her temple.

Today, very little remains of its former glory, and although the ruins of the City of Ephesus receive many thousands of visitors daily, the temple site - which is nearby - is visited by only a handful. The site's history as a temple to the Magna Mater predates the Archaic Greek period. Evidence indicates that the cult of the Greek Artemis absorbed several goddesses who were worshipped there. These include the goddess Hekate, the Anatolian Goddess Hannahanna, the Phrygian Mother Goddess Kybele, and the Persian Anahita. Earlier depictions of Artemis hint at connections with each of these goddesses.

There is evidence of human occupation of the site dating back to the neolithic period 6000 BCE, as well as a Mycenaean graveyard at the place where the Basilica of St John now stands in Selçuk, dating to around 1450 BCE showing that the site was in use. In the Classical Greek era (500 - 400 BCE), it held a position as one of the twelve cities of the Ionian League. It is possible that religious worship on the site dates to the Bronze Age (3300-1200 BCE) and

---

21 *Hyginus, Fabulae 223, circa 2nd century CE.*
22 Pausanias 4.31.7.

may have origins with the Hittite or earlier Hattic cultures who worshipped an Earth Goddess and the Sky God. If this is true, then this first temple at Ephesus was built on the site of an older shrine or sanctuary before 1000 BCE.

FIGURE 4 – THE COLOSSAL ARTEMIS, SELCUK MUSEUM.

FIGURE 5 – TURRET CROWN OF THE COLOSSAL ARTEMIS.

## Meaning of 'Ephesus'

The origin of the name of the city Ephesus has been the subject of much debate. Suggestions that it may derive from *bee*, via the Latin *apis* is interesting, but this is rejected as the history of this city predates that of the Roman influence. It is more likely that Ephesus derives from the Hittite name *Apasa*, the name of an earlier capital city of an ancient alliance *Arzarwa* in western Anatolia. If this is correct, we can date the name back to around the 14th century BCE, with inscriptions referring to it as a place of religious worship.

The city of Apasa stood just a few miles southwest of Selçuk, the modern city where the little that remains of the Ephesian temple can still be found.

## The Founding Myth: A Fish & a Boar

The historian Herodotus told of the founding of the city of Ephesus around 1000 BCE following advice from the Delphic Oracle of Apollo. Androklos, the son of King Kodors of Athens, went to Anatolia, having been told, "*A fish and a boar will show you the place*". While his men prepared a fire to cook a fish they had caught, nearby bushes caught flame, scaring a boar hiding in them. Androklos pursued the boar and killed it. He subsequently remembered the words of the Oracle and built the city of Ephesus on the killing site.

This temple was destroyed and rebuilt several times in its history. Strabo wrote that the temple underwent construction and destruction seven times. While lacking evidence to fully support this claim, archaeologists have discovered proof of the temple being reconstructed at least four times.

Pausanius claimed that the importance given to Artemis was due in part to the fame of the Amazons (a group of warrior women) who he believed dedicated the cult image and founded the city of Ephesus itself. This first temple was destroyed, possibly by flooding, and likely stood on a marshy strip of land near the river Selinus.

## King Croesus' Temple

The next temple was built around 550 BCE, paid for by the Lydian King Croesus and designed by the architect Chersiphon. This temple was famously burned to the ground in 356 BCE, allegedly on the night of the birth of Alexander the Great.

Eastern soothsayers who visited the temple prophesied that a great force capable of destroying Asia emerged into the world on the night the temple burned. We can't prove that the dates are accurate, but this story held significant mythic weight in the temple's history and that of Alexander. His mother, Olympias, may have orchestrated this narrative as a strategic manoeuvre to amplify Alexander's popularity and authority, similar to other myths surrounding his birth. For instance, a rumour circulated that Olympias shared her bed with snakes before marrying Philip II, King of Macedonia and that Alexander's father was in fact the gods Zeus or Ammon – rather than Philip II.

The arsonist responsible for setting the temple on fire, was a man named Herostratus, who was driven solely by his desire to immortalize his name. He succeeded in his endeavour, and his name continues to be spoken and written wherever the history of this temple is discussed – including this reference here. Plutarch wrote of this incident, saying that the goddess Artemis was too busy taking care of the birth of Alexander to send help to her threatened temple.

## One of the Seven Wonders of the Ancient World

In 334 BCE, Alexander proposed funding the temple's reconstruction following his conquest of Asia Minor. Nevertheless, the Ephesians, who highly prized their autonomy, declined his assistance. They told him that a *'god could not construct a temple for another god'*, which underscored a prevalent belief during that era that Alexander was a god in human form, or at the least, that he was the offspring of a god. It also cleverly served as a means to evade relinquishing political authority.

FIGURE 6 - THE SITE OF THE TEMPLE OF ARTEMIS OF EPHESUS IN 2022.

The Temple was eventually rebuilt in 323 BCE, becoming one of the Seven Wonders of the Ancient World. It was destroyed by Goths in 262 CE, looted, and most of the marble was carried away over the following decades.

## Princess Clymena

The early text of the *Etymologicum Magnum* details an intriguing story about the origins of a practice found at Ephesus. It is the story of Princess Clymena.

Clymena carried a statue of Artemis with the help of some boys and young virgins out of the city. They set it up in a field near the sea and danced and sang around it. They wanted to offer food to the goddess but had only salt to give, so they offered the goddess salt. The subsequent year, the children did not repeat the ceremony, and the goddess punished the young participants by sending an epidemic that made them ill. To avoid further problems, the children regularly offered Artemis meals to appease her.[23]

## THE BIBLE

Artemis is also referred to in the New Testament of the Bible in the story of Paul's visit to Ephesus, which led to a riot breaking out. The story is recounted in Acts 19.

Demetrius, a silversmith who made shrines for Artemis, called all the craftsmen together to discuss the danger that Paul's ministry posed, on the one hand, to their livelihood by converting people and convincing them that gods made by human hands were not actually gods, and on the other to the reputation of the Great Goddess. Hearing this, the crowd shouted, *"Great is Artemis of the Ephesians!"* which incited the riot. Paul's travelling companions, Gaius and Aristarchus, were taken to safety in the theatre, and Paul's disciples and the local officials all tried to stop Paul from entering the theatre. Attempts to silence the crowd resulted in *"Great is Artemis of the Ephesians"* being chanted for two hours.

Eventually, a city clerk managed to silence the crowd by saying, *"Fellow Ephesians, doesn't all the world know that the city of Ephesus is the guardian of the temple of the great Artemis and of her image, which fell from heaven? Therefore, since these facts are undeniable, you ought to calm down and not do anything impulsive. You have brought these men here, though they have neither robbed temples nor blasphemed our goddess....".*

---

23 Etymologicum Magnum, 252.11.

The craftsmen were then instructed to press charges through the courts and to cease their riot.

# BEES

There is no doubt that the association of bees with the Ephesian goddess was an important one. Bees are depicted on the iconic statues of the goddess, and the oval protrusions on her body almost certainly represent bee cells, from which the bee's larvae emerge. Bees were also depicted on the coins of Ephesus – both by themselves and next to images of the Ephesian goddess, further illustrating the deep and lasting connection she had with bees.

FIGURE 7 - ARTEMIS OF EPHESUS, "THE BEAUTIFUL ARTEMIS" - STATUE IN THE MUSEUM OF EPHESUS - SELCUK.

FIGURE 8 - DETAIL SHOWING BEES AND WINGED BEINGS DEPICTED ON THE SIDE OF THE EPHESIAN ICON.

The oval protrusions on the Ephesian Artemis' chest have been speculated to be many things, including women's breasts, eggs, bull's testicles, warrior armour and necklace beads. The various symbols on the body of depictions of the Ephesian goddess are anatomically correct, and there is nothing to indicate that the protrusions are like female human breasts either. They are lower down on the body and have no nipples. The shapes also strongly resemble bee cells found in a hive, from which the bees hatch.

Strengthening this idea further, we find similar protrusions on the body of the god Zeus originating from his temple at Labruanda. Zeus of Labruanda was closely associated with the double or *labrys* axe, water, and the goddess Hekate (the temple at Labruanda is geographically close to that of Hekate's famous temple at Lagina, where the labrys was also a prominent symbol). A reference from Herodotus[24] indicates that the people who settled in this region of Caria (now part of Türkiye) may have originated as a seafaring tribe in the waters around Crete during the rule of King Minos.

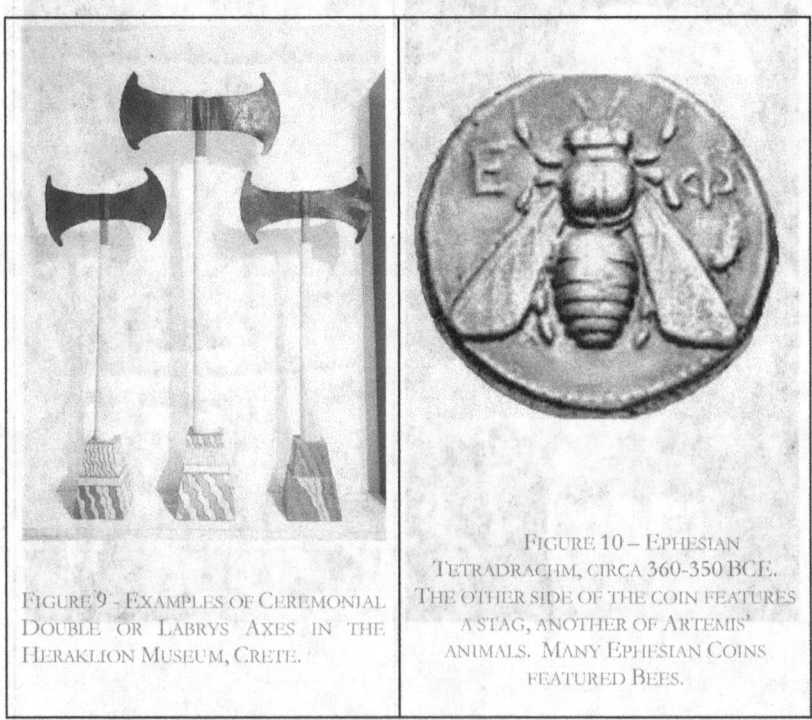

FIGURE 9 – EXAMPLES OF CEREMONIAL DOUBLE OR LABRYS AXES IN THE HERAKLION MUSEUM, CRETE.

FIGURE 10 – EPHESIAN TETRADRACHM, CIRCA 360-350 BCE. THE OTHER SIDE OF THE COIN FEATURES A STAG, ANOTHER OF ARTEMIS' ANIMALS. MANY EPHESIAN COINS FEATURED BEES.

The labrys is a prominent symbol from ancient Crete, where there is also much evidence of an unnamed female divinity with a convincing resemblance to Artemis, especially in her role as Potnia Theron. The goddess figures in Crete are associated with baetylic

---

24 Hdt. 1.171, Godley translation.

(meteoric) stones, which are also important in the cult of the Ephesian goddess.

The god Zeus has a strong connection with bees, particularly the nymph Melissa, who fed him her golden honey as an infant while being raised secretly in a cave on Crete to keep him safe from his father, Kronos. In mythology, Zeus had a son called Meliteus by a nymph. Honeybees raised Meliteus on his father's instruction after being left in the woods for dead by his mother.

FIGURE 11 - CLOSE UP OF THE OVAL SHAPES ON THE MIDRIFF OF THE EPHESIAN GODDESS.

FIGURE 12 - DETAIL FROM A SHRINE TO ZEUS LABRANDA, SHOWING THE SAME OVAL SHAPES ON HIS CHEST.

With this in mind, the protrusions on the Ephesian goddess and the Zeus of Labruanda likely represent bee cells. Proportionally, those on the body of the Ephesian goddess are smaller than those on the Labruandian Zeus – perhaps indicating the female (smaller, on the Ephesian Artemis) and the male (on Zeus) cells, respectively.

The idea that they are beads is also an interesting one, worthy of further exploration. Near Eastern deities, such as Inanna and Astarte, were also depicted with large beads around their necks. Sometimes with single, sometimes with multiple strands, and with varying quntities of beads. It is possible that the Ephesian Artemis had at least some of her roots within the same cults as theese goddesses, or that they had some shared influences. In the descent of Inanna her beads are referred to as "twin egg shaped beads" which she wears in addition to lapis lazuli beads. The Ephesian goddess' protrusion do of course also strongly resemble eggs, so that is a possibility.

The Cretan Diktynna, meaning *Sweet Virgin* or *Bee Maiden,* was also associated with bees and honey and equated to Artemis.

This depiction of the goddess spread throughout the Greek and later Roman world but significantly differs from the Greek sculptural tradition and is specific to Anatolia. It has more in common with the sculptural traditions of Assyria and Asia Minor, and maybe even Egypt, than Greece. The Greeks must have recognised functions and symbols in Ephesia as being in common with Artemis, as the Romans did later when they named her Diana.

## Priesthood

Melissa, who nurtured Zeus with honey in his cave in Crete, was said to be the first attendant of the Magna Mater, the Great Mother. Melissa is also the name given to a group of women who served the goddess at Ephesus, and we know that the Goddess worshipped at Ephesus as Artemis was equated to the Magna Mater. The early Christian writer Lactantius wrote about it in *The Divine Institute*:

> *"He [the king] had two daughters, Amalthæa and Melissa, who nourished the youthful Jupiter [i.e. Zeus] with goats' milk and honey. ... that bees flew to the child, and filled his mouth with honey. Moreover, he says that Melissa was appointed by her father the first priestess of the Great Mother; from which circumstance, the priests of the same Mother are still called Melissæ."*[25]

The text also references the Temple of Zeus at Labruanda, where the image of Zeus with similar oval protrusions as those

---

25 Lactantius, The Divine Institute, 4th century CE.

found on the chest of Artemis of Ephesus discussed above was found.

The rites and festivals of Artemis, celebrated at Ephesus, spread throughout the ancient world. Pausanias mentions an image of Artemis Ephesia in the government offices of Megalopolis[26], a statue of Artemis Ephesia in the marketplace of Corinthos[27], and a sanctuary for Artemis Ephesia in the village of Alea in Arcadia.[28] These are all in the Peloponnese, Greece.

Strabo refers to a temple of Artemis Ephesia at Massilia (Marseilles) in Gaul[29] (France), and also that the Iberians (modern Spain) practised the sacred rites of Artemis Ephesia.[30] The temple at Massilia included a reproduction of the cult statue of Ephesus after Artemis appeared to the noblewoman Aristarkha in a dream. Artemis instructed her to take a copy of the statue with her to Massilia, which she did. In acknowledgement of this, she was subsequently appointed the priestess of Artemis at Massilia.[31]

The importance of Ephesus is further stressed by Strabo when he mentions that this was the only Ionian temple not burned down and destroyed by the Persian King Xerxes when he invaded the area.[32]

# ARTEMIS OF BRAURON

The temple of Artemis Brauronia stood on what Euripides may have been referring to as the *holy stairs of Brauron* in his play, Iphigeneia in Tauris. People sometimes called it *The Parthenon of the Bear Maidens*, referring to one of its most famous rites. It is said to have been one of the twelve ancient cities of Attica, which eventually became unified with Athens.

Votive offerings dating to the 9th and 8th centuries BCE have been found at the site, suggesting that early worship of the goddess

---

26 Pausanias 8.30.6.
27 Pausanias 2.2.6.
28 Pausanias 8.23.1, see also 7.22.6 and 10.26.6.
29 Strabo 4.1.8.
30 Strabo 4.1.5.
31 Strabo 4.1.4.
32 Strabo 14.1.5.

at Brauron focused on the sacred spring and cave, which later became part of the temple complex. Evidence indicates that the site was occupied from the Neolithic period to the Late Bronze Age.

A special series of cult vessels called krateriskoi have been excavated at Brauron. These were used for dedications to Artemis. They depict naked girls running, as well as part of a bear, all perhaps pictorial renderings of the Brauronian rituals. A pit containing small votive offerings and geometric potsherds has also been unearthed.

The stone temple on the site was built around the 6th century BCE by the Athenian ruler Peisistratus or possibly by his sons. Peisistratus also established an additional sanctuary for Artemis Brauronia in the Acropolis. He incorporated many Brauronian rites into Athenian public life, further emphasising the importance of the temple at Brauron and increasing the prominence of Artemis in Athens. The remains of the stoa to Artemis Brauronia can still be seen amongst the ruins of the Acropolis today.

An official site inspection list from the 3rd century BCE provides evidence that the site included a temple, a Parthenon, stables, a wrestling school and a gymnasium. The temple was flooded later in the 3rd century BCE by the river Eurasinos and abandoned. Nine centuries later, builders erected a Christian basilica of St. George on the ruins near the sacred well.

## Foundation Myth & Icon

Some believed that Iphigeneia established the temple at Brauron. According to various accounts, King Agamemnon, the father of Iphigeneia, was murdered by his wife. Orestes, the brother of Iphigeneia, took revenge for the death of his father by killing his mother. To make amends with the gods for this act, an oracle instructed him to steal the cult statue of Artemis from the Scythians in Tauris. What Orestes did not know was that his sister Iphigeneia had been taken to Tauris by Artemis. He was caught and brought before his sister to be sacrificed to the goddess. Iphigeneia recognised her brother and helped him escape; as they fled, they stole and took the statue.

Pausanias wrote of a legend in which Iphigeneia left the wooden image of Artemis Tauropolos at Brauron when she and Orestes fled from the Taureans.[33] In another passage, he wrote that he believed the statue was taken to and installed at Limnaion, where Orestes was king, and the goddess was worshipped as Artemis Orthia.[34] He also referred to the sanctuary of Artemis Brauronia at the Acropolis,[35] from which the Persian king Xerxes stole the image when he attacked Athens.[36]

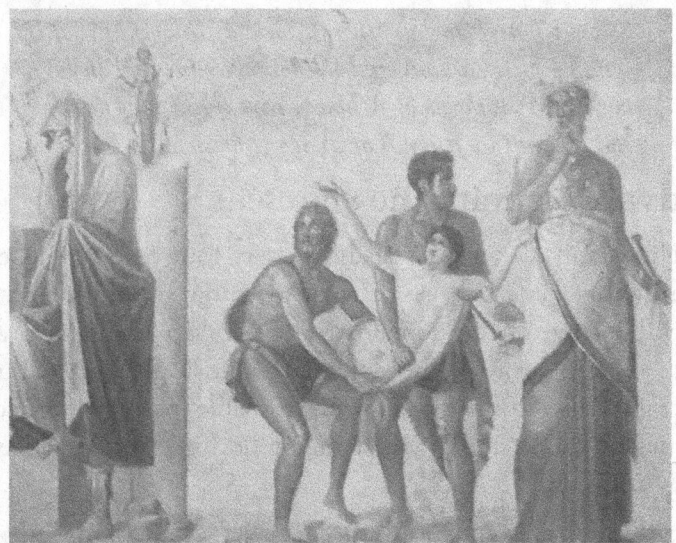

FIGURE 13 - PAINTING SHOWING A SCENE FROM THE SACRIFICE OF IPHIGENEIA'S SACRIFICE FOUND AT THE HOUSE OF THE TRAGIC POET IN THE BURIED REMAINS OF THE ROMAN CITY OF POMPEII.

## Devotion

At the temple in Brauron, Artemis' followers worshipped her as a goddess of protection during childbirth and of female children until puberty. Women who travelled from afar to make offerings to Artemis at Brauron for protection during childbirth would dedicate prized possessions to the goddess with a set of clothing following a successful birth. Gems, mirrors and rings have been recovered from the spring and the stream at Brauron. These votive offerings

---

33 Pausanias 1.33.1.
34 Pausanias 3.16.7.
35 Pausanias 1.23.7.
36 Pausanias 8.46.3.

emphasise the importance placed on the help Artemis could give in these matters.

The clothes of women who died in childbirth were offered to Iphigeneia at a shrine near the main temple at Brauron. This may link to the idea that Artemis transformed Iphigeneia into Hekate. Hekate presides over the restless dead, and women who die in childbirth may sometimes have fallen into this category.

> *"Now I have heard another account of Iphigenia that is given by Arkadians and I know that Hesiod, in his poem A Catalogue of Women, says that Iphigenia did not die, but by the will of Artemis became Hekate."*[37]

## Festival & Dancing the She-Bear

The Brauronia festival was held every four years at the temple, primarily for women. Much of what we know about it comes from images depicted on the remains of pottery fragments and vessels found in and around the sanctuary. Aristophanes, the comic playwright, also provides us with valuable passages concerning activities at this temple, which might be based on practices and beliefs of his time.[38]

Several images from Brauron depict young girls. They are shown sometimes as being naked and at others as wearing hunting tunics. Many images show the girls dancing or running near an altar, sometimes bearing torches, twigs or crowns of leaves. The girls are also often depicted in saffron-coloured robes known as *Krokotoi*.

There are differing opinions regarding the age range of the girls who went to Brauron. Some writers suggest that they were around five to ten years old; others indicate that girls went there during puberty, after which they would be ready to marry and be dedicated to the goddesses Hera and Aphrodite. In the Lysistrata, a woman recounts how she took the role of the she-bear at Brauron at the age of ten.[39]

---

37 Description of Greece, Pausanias, 2nd century CE, trans. Jones, 1918.
38 Peace 872-6 and Lysistrata 638f.
39 Aristophanes, Lysistrata 638.

Some images show a fire burning on the altar. Some fragments show the use of twigs for sprinkling water from chalices, implying ritual lustration - likewise, the sacrifice of a goat to the goddess.

During the festival, young girls participated in the ceremonies as Arktoi, meaning she-bear. This custom originates in a story that tells of the killing of a tame she-bear who frequented the sanctuary. A young girl teased the she-bear, which became agitated. It attacked the girl and ripped out her eye. Subsequently, the girl's brothers take revenge on the bear, killing it. Artemis retaliates and sends a plague to the sanctuary. In desperation, the people of Brauron consult an oracle for help, who tells them to appease the goddess by letting young girls take the role of the she-bear in a mystery play.

It may have been that the she-bear that was killed was previously involved in some of the festivities at Brauron and that the girls replaced the bear's role. However, it is equally possible that this element of the story may have been a completely new addition to the rituals to honour the bear that had been killed.

Although it was said that all Athenian girls had to dance the she-bear at Brauron before marriage, it would have only been possible for a privileged few.

The act of dancing the she-bear before marriage could also be seen as representing an initiatory rite of passage experience, marking the transition from childhood to womanhood. The dance itself could represent the transformation of the girls from the wild and untamed status of childhood, to that of a respectable life as a married woman.

## Other Rites

Newlywed girls would dedicate their virginal robes to Artemis as an offering, thanking the goddess for protecting their virginity[40]. Upon marriage, they rededicated themselves to Hera, the goddess of marriage and Aphrodite, the goddess of sensual love.

---

40 Suidas, Lysizonos gune.

## Boys at Brauron

Statues and other depictions of young boys have also been found at Brauron. We can speculate that boys were allowed to join the temple if they were part of a girl-boy twin, reflecting the divine relationship of Artemis to her twin brother Apollo.

# TEMPLES OF ARTEMIS BY REGION

From ancient records, we know of temples and sanctuaries dedicated to Artemis throughout the ancient Greek world. What follows is a list of the best known temples based on region. There may well be more to add to this list – as Artemis' worship continued not only for a very long time but also in a very wide geographic region:

## Central Greece

Central Greece was divided into several regions, and home to many temples to Artemis. We know of temples located at Amarynthos, Amphissa, Antikyra, Artemision, Aulis, Boulis, Calydon, Delphi, Hyampolis, Kirrha, Kyrtones, Lilaia, Naupaktos, Oiantheia, Plataia, Tanagra and Thebes.

## Southern Greece

The largest number of known temples and groves dedicated to Artemis were located in southern Greece. There were also temples on the islands of Aigina and Salamis off the southern Greek coast. Temples and groves of Artemis existed at Aigeira, Aigion, Akakesion, Alagonia, Alea, Amyklai, Argos, Athens, Athmonia, the Azanian Hills, Boiai, Brauron, Corinthos, Dereion, Eleusis, Elis, Epidauros, Epidauros Limera, Helos, Hermione, Hypsous, Kaphya, Karyai, Korone, Letrinoi, Limnai, Lousoi, Lykoa, Marios, Megalopolis, Megara, Messene, Mothone, Mount Artemisios, Mount Koryphon, Mount Krathis, Mount Lykone, Mounykhia, Myrrhinos, Olympia, Oresthasion, Orkhomenos, Orneai, Pagai, Patrai, Pellene, Phelloi, Pheneos, Phigalia, Phlya, Pisa, Pyrrhikhos, Sikyon, Skias, Skillos, Sparta (including a shrine on the road to Arcadia), Stymphalos, Tegea, Teuthis, Teuthrone, Trikolonoi, Troizenos, Zoitea and Zoster.

## Northern Greece

There are only two references to Artemis' temples in northern Greece, which were at Melite and Pherai in Thessalia.

## The Aegean Sea

Many of the islands in the Aegean Sea had temples to Artemis on them. These include Delos in the Cyclades Islands (famous as the place of her birth), the Hekatonnesoi Islands, Ikaria, Samos, Rhodes and Crete.

## Türkiye

There were also many temples to Artemis in what is now Türkiye. A large number of towns and villages with sacred shrines or temples to Artemis in Türkiye included Adrasteia, Astyra, Bargylia, Bubastos, Byzantion, Didim, Ephesus, Hypoplakinan Thebes, Kalydna, Kastabos, Korakios, Lake Gygaia, Magnesia, Miletos & Didyma, Mount Sipylos, Ortygia, Perge, Phrygia, Pitane, Pygela and Pylai.

## Greek Colonies

When the Greeks travelled and traded, they took their deities with them. As a result, there were also temples around the Mediterranean and up into Scythia (modern Ukraine and nearby regions). Artemis temples at Greek colonies stood at Khersonesos in Scythia, Iberia (modern Spain), Massilia (Marseilles) in Southern Gaul (modern France), Capua and the Henetoi regions of Italy, and Syracuse in Sikelia (Sicily).

# 4.
# FESTIVALS OF ARTEMIS

The ancient Greeks had a profound reverence and respect for their deities, and as such, they often celebrated them with elaborate festivals. We know that many temples held celebrations with a local and that festivals and religious rites took place at many of the smaller shrines and sanctuaries. Although archaeological remains provide valuable evidence regarding temples and accompanying religious imagery, determining the festivals' specific timing and intricate details remains challenging due to the scarcity of available evidence. However, despite this limitation, the abundance of diverse sources, including specific textual references, enables us to glean significant insights into the nature and scope of these ancient celebrations.

To complicate things even more, those who lived in and around the ancient Greek world did not have one universally accepted calendar; instead, each state had their own, based on a lunisolar calendar. As the name suggests, lunisolar calendars take into account both solar and lunar cycles – which in turn makes it nearly impossible to accurately attribute festival dates to a modern calendar as the dates will be different each year in our Gregorian calendar.

Illustrating the importance of Artemis' festivals, we find that in the Attic calendar (as used in Athens), there were two Spring months named after Artemis: *Artemis Elaphebolos* and *Artemis Mounykhia*. The Attic calendar consisted of the months Hekatombaion, Metageitnion, Boedromion, Pyanopsion, Maimakterion, Poseidon, Gamelion, Anethesterion, Elaphebolion, Mounykhion, Thargelion and Skirophorion.

In Delos, the calendar shared some names with the Attic calendar. The sequence of months there was Hekatombaion, Metageitnion, Bouphonion, Apatourion, Aresion, Poseideon, Lenaion, Hieros, Galaxion, Artemision, Thargelion and Panemos. They named Artemision in honour of Artemis.

Festivals and rites were held at many of Artemis' temples and sanctuaries, such as the famous Brauronia festival held every four years in Brauron.[41] The festivals of Artemis described in most detail by ancient writers are the Brauronia, Charisteria, Elaphebolia, Hiketeria, Laphria, Mounykhia and Thargelia.

## FROM THE RECORDS

Ancient writers like Pausanias mentioned some festivals in passing, who probably expected their audience to be familiar with these ceremonies. As a result, while we have the names of some of the festivals, we don't always have much in the way of practical details of what the celebrations entailed.

From Pausanias, we know that annual festivals were held for Artemis Daphnaií (of the laurel or bay tree) and Artemis Elaphiaia (of the deer) at Olympia. He mentions a festival held for Artemis Hymnia (of the hymns) on the border of Orkhomenos in Arcadia, where priests of Artemis lived their lives in purity, abstaining from sex, ritualised washing and never entering private homes. He also recorded an annual festival for Artemis Diktynna (of the nets, i.e. fishing nets) that was held at the temple in Hypsous, Lacedaemon.

Pausanias mentions an annual Saronia festival[42], but we know little about it. Saronia refers to an Argosian hero, Saron, who established a sanctuary in honour of Artemis near Troizenos in Argolis, where this festival was held.[43]

Xenophon recorded a festival when he wrote that a failed attack on Thebes took place on the last day of the festival of Artemis Eukleia (Glory and Good Repute) in 392 BCE.

Hesychius wrote about female dancers from Sparta who danced at a festive celebration for Artemis Koryphaia (from the name of the mountain near Argos).

---

41 See, chapter 3 - Temples & Sanctuaries of Artemis.
42 Pausanias 2.32.10.
43 Pausanias 2.32.10.

# CHARISTERIA

Charisteria, meaning *thanksgiving*, took place on the 6th Boedromion and honoured the victory over the Persians at Marathon. At this festival, five hundred goats were sacrificed to the goddess Artemis Agrotera (huntress, or of the wilds) and the god Ares Enyalios (warlike). The goats were taken to the temple of Artemis Agrotera on the Ilissos in a ceremonial procession and then sacrificed. The Athenians initially offered a goat for every Persian slain. However, due to the number of Persians they killed, they realised that doing so would wipe out the entire goat population, so they settled on five hundred instead.

This sanctuary was unique amongst Artemis shrines in that it was dedicated to Artemis and the war god Ares rather than to her and her brother Apollo. The reason for this is unclear; however, the Amazons likely connected the dedication to the worship of Artemis and Ares.

# ELAPHEBOLIA

Hyampolis in Phocis was renowned for celebrating the Elaphebolia, a famous and widely celebrated festival. At Phocis, the festival was held on the 6th Elaphebolion and celebrated the victory of the townspeople over the Thessalians who had ravaged the countryside surrounding them.

Elaphos cakes were made of dough, honey and sesame seeds during the festival. The cakes, likely made in the shape of a stag or deer, were offered to Artemis Elaphebolos during the festivities.

Elaphos cakes are also mentioned by Herodotus when he wrote about three hundred Corcyraean boys who were sent to Alyattes to be made eunuchs. When they stopped at Samos, the locals encouraged them to take sanctuary in the temple of Artemis. The Corinthians, who forbade the Samians from bringing food into the temple so that they could starve the boys into submission, were furious. The Samians responded by inventing a new festival to Artemis to save the children. Each night, choirs of young boys and girls circled the temple with cakes of sesame and honey in their hands, which the Corcyraean boys could grab. The cakes allowed them to survive and were a fitting gesture of defiance in celebration of a goddess who protects the young. The Corinthians eventually gave up, and the Samians returned the boys to their homes. This invented festival continued and is thought to be the source of the Elaphebolia festival.[44]

# HIKETERIA

Plutarch, in his Life of Thesus, records that on the 6th Mounykhion, a procession of virgin girls would walk to the Delphinion (the name given to shrines to the Delphinian Apollo, the God of Oracles), each carrying an olive twig bound with white wool.[45] Although there is no clear record of the name of this festival, it may have been called Hiketeria[46] after the suppliant's twigs carried by the girls (hiketeria). The twigs may have served an apotropaic function as a charm to protect from evil things.

We know that the sixth day of the month was sacred to Artemis, so it seems reasonably sure that this ceremony enacted by maiden girls was in her honour.

# LAPHRIA

The Laphria was held at Patrai and was a rather grim festival where a selection of animals were burned alive as a sacrifice. It was a significant state festival, and the main festival days were public holidays to enable everyone to participate.

Pausanias gave a detailed description of the festival in his *Description of Hellas*, recording his observations saying that around the altar, a circle of logs of green wood was placed, with dry wood on the altar. Earth was piled on the altar steps to allow a smooth ascent to the altar. A procession to Artemis commenced the festival, with the officiating priestess riding in a chariot pulled by deer, imitating the golden chariot of Artemis. The following day, the central part of the festival would take place.

---

44 Herodotus, The Histories, 3.48.
45 Attische Feste – Ludwig Deubner, 1932, p201.
46 Festivals of Attica – Erica Simon, p79.

First, the fruits of cultivated trees were placed on the altar, followed by animals. The animals were thrown onto the altar while they were alive. It was then set on fire, burning the fruit offerings and the live animals. Various animals were recorded as being sacrificed in this manner at Patria, including bears, boars, deer and wolves. Any animals that tried to escape were thrown back onto the pyre.

# MOUNYKHIA

The festival of Mounykhia was celebrated on the 16th Mounykhion to Artemis at Piraeus. This full moon ceremony was sacred to Artemis-Hekate, and participants offered small cakes called amphiphontes (meaning shining on both sides). These cakes were also offered to Hekate as part of deipnon (supper) offerings at crossroads. Reference is made to little torches decorating the cakes, much like birthday cakes with small candles today. Some have speculated that these may provide clues to the origins of our modern birthday cake.[47]

Athenaios wrote that amphiphontes were offered at the temples of Artemis and at crossroads on the sixteenth of each month when the sky was lit by both the sun and the moon from either side and accordingly became amphipho.[48] Crossroads are more often associated with Hekate, and this is an additional example of how these two goddesses were conflated.

After the victory over the Persians at the sea battle of Salamis, this festival was also celebrated at Mounykhia. Even though the battle had taken place seven months earlier, Artemis's assistance in the battle was vital, and the victory was celebrated at this festival in her honour.

---

[47] Ludwig Deubner in Attische Feste and H.W. Parke in Festivals of the Athenians, 1977.
[48] Athenaios, Deipnosophistai 14.645a.

# THARGELIA

This festival, which offered the first fruits, took place on the 6th and 7th of Thargelion and marked the birthdays of Artemis and Apollo respectively.

On the festival's first day, two people would be selected from the poor to become scapegoats. They would be given a feast of food, after which they were ritually beaten, representing the city's purification. The next day, offerings of the first fruits, or *thargelos*, were made to the gods.

The ritual offerings were followed by hymn-singing contests in which the men and boys participated.

# 5.
# MYTHS & LEGENDS

Artemis was undoubtedly one of the most significant of the ancient Greek deities, and this is reflected by the frequency of her appearances in myths, literature, and art, as well as the considerable number of temples and shrines dedicated to her. Mythology provides clues to the different attributes of the goddess.

The following section provides summaries of the roles she played in some of the ancient myths, indicating some of her strengths and weaknesses. These myths also illustrate Artemis's relationships with other deities, including Zeus, Dionysus, Apollo and Leto.

## THE ALOADAI GIANTS

The Aloadai giants were young twins described as fifty-four feet high and eighteen feet across. At the age of nine, they decided to fight the Olympian gods. They had already demonstrated their strength by capturing the war god Ares and chaining him in a brazen cauldron for thirteen months. Hermes rescued Ares when Eriboia, the stepmother of the giants, revealed Ares' location.[49]

To attack the Olympian gods, the young giants placed Mount Ossa on top of Mount Olympus, then placed Mount Pelion on top of Mount Ossa, creating a tower to the sky to reach the gods. The first Olympians they encountered on their raid were the goddesses Artemis and Hera. The first twin, Ephialtes, tried to force his unwanted attention on Hera, and the second Otos did likewise to Artemis. Artemis escaped Otos by shapeshifting into a deer, distracting the young giants. Unwisely, Ephialtes and Otos then decided they wanted to kill this divine deer. They tried to spear her, but Artemis cunningly ran between them, moving too swiftly for the cumbersome giants to hit her. As a result, they missed and killed each other instead, just as she had planned.[50] The giants die at

---

49 Iliad 5.385.
50 Apollodorus, The Library 1.53.

Naxos, where Dionysus subsequently meets Ariadne after her abandonment by the hero Theseus.

# THE HYPERBOREOI

Artemis was the patron deity of the mythical Hyperboreoi with her brother Apollo. The Hyperboreoi were said to be a race of long-lived men living in a realm of eternal spring in the far north. They are mentioned in connection with Medea, who refers to them in Thessalia when speaking to King Pelias of Iolkos.

Medea, the daughter of King Aeetes[51], was a devotee of the goddess Hekate. The princess was an accomplished enchantress and caused dragons to appear in the sky over Thessalia through the use of hallucinogenic drugs. She also declared that they had brought the goddess from Hyperborea to visit his land.[52]

Artemis appears to have favoured the Hyperboreans, as she appointed several as temple attendants. For example, she immortalized the three maidens Hekaerge, Loxo and Oupis to be attendants of the shrine on the island of Delos.

The virgins Arge and Opis, attendants at the temple of Artemis on Delos, were also said to come from Hyperborea.[53] In one version of the Orion tale, Artemis shoots him for trying to force his attention onto Opis.[54] Ritual begging was practised in their names on Delos.

As a curious aside, Apollo was said to take a holiday from his Oracle at Delphi and his duties elsewhere, spending it in Hyperborea. While Apollos is away, the god Dionysus takes his place at Delphi.

---

51 King Aeetes, with his sisters Circe and Pasiphae were said to be the children of the Sun God Helios, so Medea was both semi-divine and of an important royal lineage.
52 Diodorus Siculus 4.50.6.
53 Herodotus 4.35.1.
54 Apollodorus 1.27.

# THE INDIAN WARS OF DIONYSUS

The Dionysiaca (circa 5th century CE) describes a conflict known as the Indian Wars of Dionysus. In this story, some Greek Gods were fighting each other in India, one side led by Dionysus, the beautiful god of wine and wildness and the other by Hera, queen of the gods. During this conflict, Artemis fought on the side of Dionysus.

This story emphasises Artemis' friendship with Dionysus and her continued rivalry and dislike of Hera. When Hera and Artemis met in combat, Hera took advantage of her position as Zeus's wife. As Artemis was shooting her arrows at Hera, Hera seized one of Zeus' clouds and used it as a shield, absorbing all the arrows. Artemis eventually ran out of arrows, at which point Hera picked a large chunk of hail out of the air and threw it at Artemis, breaking her bow. Hera threw a second chunk of hail at Artemis, hitting her on the chest and knocking her over.[55]

Artemis also tried to save Dionysus when, at Hera's command, he was driven mad by one of the Furies. Again, Hera managed to triumph over Artemis, this time by throwing a burning torch at her, forcing her away and preventing her from helping Dionysus. She did, however, prevent wild beasts from harming the delirious god.[56]

# THE SACRIFICE OF IPHIGENEIA

The story of Iphigeneia tells of a young girl who became a mortal attendant of Artemis, who the goddess later turns into an immortal. She could likely be an earlier goddess associated with childbirth, as her name might mean *she who is born with force*. Although in the myths she is the daughter of King Agamemnon, later sources, such as Antoninus Liberalis[57] claimed that she was the daughter of Perseus and Helen. The story, which played an essential role in the Trojan War was written about by many Greek and later Roman writers, with slight variations in the versions presented.

---

55 Dionysiaca 36.28.
56 Dionysiaca 32.100-118.
57 Antoninus Liberalis, Metamorphoses, 27.

The story starts with King Agamemnon offending Artemis by boasting that he was the most excellent hunter after killing a deer. His arrogance angered Artemis, who punished his hubris by causing the wind to be still and preventing his fleet from sailing. The soothsayer Kalkhas subsequently informed Agamemnon that Artemis would not allow him to sail until he offered his most beautiful daughter, Iphigeneia, as a sacrifice to Artemis to appease her.

In Aeschylus' Agamemnon, the goddess demanded the sacrifice of Iphigeneia because she was angry that an eagle near the palace of Agamemnon killed a pregnant hare. This was also said to be an omen for the destruction of Troy, with the hare representing Troy and the eagle the avenging Greeks. Agamemnon placed Iphigeneia on the altar, but at the last moment, Artemis replaced the girl with a deer, taking her to safety and appointing her as a priestess instead. According to an account by Apollodorus, some claimed that Artemis made her immortal.[58] In the version told by Ovid in his Metamorphoses, Iphigeneia offered herself as a willing sacrifice by lying down on the altar. The Priests and Agamemnon all wept at the thought of losing her. Artemis was pleased by the girl's courage, brought a mist over the proceedings, took Iphigeneia in the turmoil of the ritual and left a hind in her place.

When the same story is recounted by Antoninus Liberalis, Artemis placed a bull on the altar, carrying Iphigeneia to the Sea of Pontos. Iphigeniea names the tribe she finds there, the Taureans, after the bull sacrificed in her place.[59] Following this, we see the roots of the founding of the Artemis shrine at Brauron when Iphigeneia and her brother Orestes took the cult statue of Artemis from Tauros to Brauron.

Iphigeneia was sometimes subsumed into the figure of the goddess Hekate, and Hesiod tells us that Artemis transformed the girl into Hekate:

---

58 Apollodorus E3.21.
59 Antoninus Liberalis, Metamorphoses, 27.

> "Hesiod in the Catalogues of Women represented that Iphigeneia was not killed but, by the will of Artemis, became Hekate."[60]

## CALLISTO'S FALL

Callisto (or Kallisto) was a princess of Lycaon, Arcadia. She loved hunting and joined Artemis as a companion, swearing to be virginal forever and eternally loyal to Artemis. However, when Zeus saw Callisto, he desired her and forced himself on her, impregnating her. In some versions of the tale, he assumed the form of Artemis to get close to Callisto before molesting her.[61]

Callisto tried to hide her pregnancy from Artemis, managing to do so for a while. However, while Artemis and her companions bathed, the goddess noticed Callisto's growing belly and became furious with her. According to Hesiod, the outraged Artemis turned the girl into a bear, hunting and killing her.[62]

Apollodorus recounts a slightly different version of the story, in which Zeus changed Callisto into a bear to protect her from Artemis and Hera. However, Hera persuaded Artemis to shoot Callisto in her bear form. Apollodorus also mentioned that some claimed Artemis killed Callisto for failing to preserve her virginity. As Callisto died, Zeus took the unborn baby and gave it to Maia to rear in Arcadia, calling it *Arkas* (meaning *bear*).[63]

Both versions tell us that Zeus, mourning the death of Callisto, placed her amongst the stars, naming the constellation Arktos. Arktos is the constellation we know as *Ursa Major*, meaning *Big Bear*.

## KING LYGDAMIS OF SCYTHIA

King Lygdamis of Scythia must have been foolish, mad or both when he threatened to take his army and lay waste to the shrine of Artemis at Ephesus. Artemis protected her shrine by demonstrating

---

60 Catalogues of Women Frag 71 (from Pausanias 1.43.1).
61 E.g. in the Dionysiaca.
62 Hesiod, The Astronomy Frag 3 (Pseudo-Eratosthenes, Catasterismi Frag 1.2).
63 Apollodorus 3.100.

her ability to strike from afar with her arrows of disease, protecting what was dear to her. Before the King and his army reached Ephesus, the goddess struck them down with a deadly plague, and they all died.[64]

## QUEEN NIOBE OF THEBES

Queen Niobe of Thebes, daughter of King Tantalus, was a proud woman who did not pay due respect to the gods. She had seven sons and seven daughters with her husband Amphion, who grew up to be beautiful young men and women. One day, at a ceremony in honour of the goddess Leto, Queen Niobe was heard boasting that she was more blessed than Leto, who only had one son and one daughter. Leto, hearing this insult, became enraged. In her anger, Leto instructed Artemis and Apollo to slay all the daughters and sons of Niobe. The twins slew the sons and daughters of Niobe, with Artemis killing the daughters and Apollo the sons. They spared only one daughter, Khloris, and one son, Amyklas, who had prayed to Leto for forgiveness.[65] Pausanias tells us that Khloris was originally called Meliboia, but that due to the fright of seeing her siblings killed, she became extremely pale and remained that way, thereby gaining the name Khloris, meaning *pale one*. At the temple described by Pausanias at Argos, he stated that there was a statue of Khloris alongside that of Artemis. It is further interesting to note that Pausanias did not believe that any of Niobe's children survived, although he does recount the story nonetheless.[66]

Homer, who recounts the story in the Iliad, wrote that Niobe's children lay unburied for nine days as Zeus turned the people to stone. On the tenth day, the gods took pity, returned the people to their normal state and allowed the children to receive appropriate burials in their tombs.

In one version, Amphion, Niobe's husband, committed suicide when he learned that his children had been massacred. In another, he was also killed by Apollo when he attempted to avenge the death

---

64 Callimachus, Hymn 3 to Artemis.
65 Diodorus Siculus 4.74.3., Pausanias 2.21.9.
66 Pausanias 2.21.9.

of his children. Pausanias writes that Amphion was further punished after his death by Hades, the god of the underworld, for mocking Leto.[67] Niobe, grieving the loss of her children, fled to Mount Sipylos in Asia Minor, where she turned into a weeping rock. The endless tears from the stone formed a stream, the Achelous. In the Dionysiaca, it is suggested that it might be Nemesis, the goddess of divine vengeance, who turned Niobe to stone.[68]

In the Iliad[69], Homer wrote that Niobe *"stands among the crags in the untrodden hills of Sipylos, where people say the Nymphs, when they have been dancing on the banks of Achelous, lay themselves down to sleep. There Niobe, in marble, broods on the desolation that the gods dealt out to her."* On Mount Sipylos is a limestone rock, which is said to be Queen Niobe. The stone, which resembles the shape of a woman, is said to weep due to how water seeps through it, forming droplets. It is known as the Weeping Rock.

## THE SLAYING OF ORION

There are conflicting stories about the relationship between the giant Orion and Artemis. In some, Orion is a hunting companion of Artemis, who gets killed by Gaia's scorpion for boasting that he could kill anything on the earth. In other versions, Artemis and Orion seem to have a friendlier relationship.

Ovid states that the scorpion initially attempted to kill Leto, but Orion intervened to protect Leto and lost his life due to doing so. Leto then placed him amongst the stars as a reward for saving her life.[70]

Apollodorus recounts how Artemis killed Orion on Delos, where Aphrodite took him. Apollodorus gave two possible reasons for this killing: either Orion challenged Artemis to a discus match (presumably claiming to be better than the goddess) or because he forced himself on Opis, one of Artemis' virgin attendants.[71] A Roman version of the story, which centres around the creation of

---

67 Pausanias 9.5.9.
68 Dionysiaca 48.395.
69 Iliad 24:612ff.
70 Ovid, Fasti 5.493.
71 Apollodorus 1.25.

the constellation of Scorpio, substitutes the goddess Diana for Artemis and introduces a romantic element. This story, which Hyginus recounted in his Astronomica, tells the story of how Tellus (Gaia) sent the scorpion (Scorpio) to kill Orion for boasting to Diana (Artemis) and Latona (Leto) that he could kill anything the Earth produced.

Following the death of Orion, Jove (Zeus) placed the Scorpion amongst the stars in remembrance of the courage of both parties and as a lesson to humanity not to be too full of self-confidence. Diana (Artemis), mourning the loss of Orion, asked Jove (Zeus) to grant her the same favour as he had given to Tellus (Gaia). For this reason, Jove (Zeus) created the Orion constellation so that it would set in the night sky whenever Scorpio rose.[72]

In another version of this story, Hyginus writes that Istrus said that Diana (Artemis) loved Orion and that the two considered getting married. Apollo, brother to Diana, did not take this lightly and tried to dissuade her, but to no avail. Apollo then tricked her into shooting Orion. He dares her that she could not hit a distant black object in the sea with her arrows. The object was Orion swimming in the distance. Proud and confident of her shooting skills, she shoots a single arrow, killing Orion. His body later washed up upon the shore, and Diana, grieving his loss, placed him amongst the stars as the constellation of Orion.[73]

---

[72] Hyginus, Astronomica 2.26.
[73] Hyginus, Astronomica 2.34.

# 6.
# TITLES OF ARTEMIS

Artemis had numerous cult titles or epithets in addition to the name *Artemis*. These names can provide us with more insight into the goddess, as they give us a clearer perception of which of her qualities were most focused on and emphasised by her worshippers.

Epithets are additional names given to a deity which convey information about them. They usually describe a quality the deity possesses, a place or symbol they are associated with or a role they held. Epithets may also come about because of the conflation of two or more deities considered the equivalent or otherwise similar enough to be considered the same. Naturally, hundreds of words might be regarded as epithets of a goddess like Artemis, whose worship was spread over a long period and geographical region and enjoyed tremendous popularity. The following list illustrates some of the better-known and more widely used epithets.

## ADRASTEIA Αδράστεια

Suidas referenced Demetrios of Skepsis, saying that a king named Adrastos established the cult of Artemis *Adrasteia* at Troas in northwest Anatolia. Here, the meaning of Adrasteia, would imply *of Adrastos*.

King Adrastos was also credited with building a temple to the goddess Nemesis, with whom the name Adrasteia is associated. Adrasteia was worshipped as a goddess of *inevitable fate* in her own right and conflated with Artemis, as well as with Kybele, and Rhea.

## AGORAIA Αγοραία

Pausanias refers to an altar of Artemis *Agoraia*, meaning *of the marketplace*, at the village of Olympia.[74]

---

[74] Pausanias 5.15.4.

the constellation of Scorpio, substitutes the goddess Diana for Artemis and introduces a romantic element. This story, which Hyginus recounted in his Astronomica, tells the story of how Tellus (Gaia) sent the scorpion (Scorpio) to kill Orion for boasting to Diana (Artemis) and Latona (Leto) that he could kill anything the Earth produced.

Following the death of Orion, Jove (Zeus) placed the Scorpion amongst the stars in remembrance of the courage of both parties and as a lesson to humanity not to be too full of self-confidence. Diana (Artemis), mourning the loss of Orion, asked Jove (Zeus) to grant her the same favour as he had given to Tellus (Gaia). For this reason, Jove (Zeus) created the Orion constellation so that it would set in the night sky whenever Scorpio rose.[72]

In another version of this story, Hyginus writes that Istrus said that Diana (Artemis) loved Orion and that the two considered getting married. Apollo, brother to Diana, did not take this lightly and tried to dissuade her, but to no avail. Apollo then tricked her into shooting Orion. He dares her that she could not hit a distant black object in the sea with her arrows. The object was Orion swimming in the distance. Proud and confident of her shooting skills, she shoots a single arrow, killing Orion. His body later washed up upon the shore, and Diana, grieving his loss, placed him amongst the stars as the constellation of Orion.[73]

---

[72] Hyginus, Astronomica 2.26.
[73] Hyginus, Astronomica 2.34.

# 6.
# TITLES OF ARTEMIS

Artemis had numerous cult titles or epithets in addition to the name *Artemis*. These names can provide us with more insight into the goddess, as they give us a clearer perception of which of her qualities were most focused on and emphasised by her worshippers.

Epithets are additional names given to a deity which convey information about them. They usually describe a quality the deity possesses, a place or symbol they are associated with or a role they held. Epithets may also come about because of the conflation of two or more deities considered the equivalent or otherwise similar enough to be considered the same. Naturally, hundreds of words might be regarded as epithets of a goddess like Artemis, whose worship was spread over a long period and geographical region and enjoyed tremendous popularity. The following list illustrates some of the better-known and more widely used epithets.

## ADRASTEIA Αδράστεια

Suidas referenced Demetrios of Skepsis, saying that a king named Adrastos established the cult of Artemis *Adrasteia* at Troas in northwest Anatolia. Here, the meaning of Adrasteia, would imply *of Adrastos*.

King Adrastos was also credited with building a temple to the goddess Nemesis, with whom the name Adrasteia is associated. Adrasteia was worshipped as a goddess of *inevitable fate* in her own right and conflated with Artemis, as well as with Kybele, and Rhea.

## AGORAIA Αγοραία

Pausanias refers to an altar of Artemis *Agoraia*, meaning *of the marketplace*, at the village of Olympia.[74]

---

[74] Pausanias 5.15.4.

# AGROTERA Αγροτέρα

This title, meaning *the huntress* or *of the wilds*, was one of the most commonly used for Artemis in the Iliad; is also found in Pausanias.[75] It emphasizes her preference for hunting in the wilderness of mountains and forests. The temple of Artemis *Agrotera* in Athens, dated to circa 5th century BCE, had a statue of Artemis with her bow, as it was said to be the first place where she hunted when she arrived from Delos.[76] Six hundred goats were sacrificed at this temple as an offering for victory in the Battle of Marathon (490 BCE). The temple remained standing until it was destroyed in the 18th century during the Ottoman occupation.

A temple in Hyllos in Megara was also dedicated to Artemis *Agrotera* and Apollo *Agraios* (*the hunter*) by Alkathoos after killing the Kithaironian lion.[77]

The epithet *agrotera* is also used for the nymph Cyrene.

# AIGINAIÍ Αιγιναίας

There was a sanctuary at Sparta of Artemis *Aiginaií*, meaning *of Aiginia* (the island Aegina).[78] The same island was said to have a significant temple to the goddess Hekate, and there is an interesting story here that parallels other stories involving Artemis.

Diktynna, the Cretan Virgin Goddess, ran from a lusty King Minos and threw herself into the sea. She was rescued by fishermen who took her to the island of Aegina, where her cult likely continued as that of the goddess *Aphaia*.

Also see *Artemis Diktynna*.

# AITHOPIA Αιθοπία

This title, meaning *of brightness* or *burning-faced one*, was found on a statue of Artemis at her temple on the island of Lesbos.

---

[75] Pausanias 1.19.6, see also 2.3.5, & 5.15.8, & 7.26.3, & 7.26.11, & 8.32.4.
[76] Pausanias 1.19.6.
[77] Pausanias 1.41.3.
[78] Pausanias 3.14.2.

## AITOLÍ Αιτωλή

At Naupaktos in Ozolian Lokris (Nafpaktos, West Greece), there was a sanctuary of Artemis *Aitolí*, meaning *of Aitolia*. Artemis' brother Apollo shared this title here. The white marble statue there was of Artemis hurling a javelin.[79] Strabo also refers to a precinct sacred to Artemis *Aitolí* amongst the Henetoi of Northern Italy, where wild animals were said to become tame and deer herded with wolves.[80]

## ALPHEIAIA Αλφειαία

There was a sacred precinct to Artemis *Alpheiaia*, meaning *of the river Alpheios*, at the village of Letrinoi near the outlet of the river in Elis in southern Greece. Strabo describes two famous paintings there; one of Artemis borne aloft on a griffin by Aregon and another of the Capture of Troy by Kleanthes.[81]

## AMARYSIÍ Αμαρυσίη

At Amarynthos in Euboia there was a temple to Artemis *Amarysií*, meaning of *Amarynthos*, where a significant festival was celebrated in her honour.[82] Strabo describes carvings on the pillar of the temple showing the festival procession containing three thousand soldiers, six hundred horsemen and sixty chariots.[83]

## ANAEITIS Αναεῖτις/Αναῖτης

Pausanias mentions the Lydians had a shrine of Artemis *Anaeitis* and the lunar god *Mēn Tamou* but says nothing that helps explain this.[84] The god Mēn was a local Phrygian god who was also associated with the goddesses Hekate, Kybele and Anahita.

---

79 Pausanias 10.38.12.
80 Strabo 5.1.9.
81 Strabo 8.3.12.
82 Pausanias 1.31.5.
83 Strabo 10.1.10.
84 Pausanias 3.16.7.

## APANKHOMENÍ Απαγχομένη

One of the peculiar forms of Artemis is *Apankhomení*, meaning *the strangled lady*. Pausanias [85] recounts the tale of some children putting a noose around the neck of an Artemis statue, declaring that they were hanging her. In fear of retribution from Artemis, the men of the village stoned the children to death. Artemis, responded with fury towards the adults for killing the children and retaliated by sending disease to the women of the village as punishment. To appease Artemis and to atone for the wrongdoing of killing the children, the cult of the *Hanging Artemis of Kaphya*[86] in Arcadia was created.

As an aside, it is interesting to note that the maiden Aspalis committed suicide by hanging herself to preserve her virginity. This may have been a symbolic choice of death to associate herself with Artemis in this guise. Lactantius described another instance of suicide by hanging in his commentary on the Thebaid of Statius, where he describes the dancing maidens at Karyai fearing they would be sexually molested, taking shelter in a tree and hanging themselves from the branches. [87] As an aside, individuals who committed suicide were said to join the retinue of the goddess Hekate.

## ARISTE Αρίστη

Pausanias refers to a wooden image of Artemis with the epithet *Ariste*, meaning *best*, in the precinct of Artemis in Athens.[88]

## ARISTIBOULE Αριστήβουλη

Plutarch records that the Athenian leader Themistokles built a temple to Artemis *Aristiboule*, meaning *the best counsellor*.[89] Sacrifices of criminals were also made to Artemis Aristiboule. Initially, this custom was performed to Kronos on the sixth day of Metageitnion, but it was replaced with a sacrifice to Artemis (the sixth of each

---

85 Pausanias 8.23.6.
86 Orchomenos, southeast of Khotoussa.
87 Lactantius, ad Statius Thebaid, 4.225.
88 Pausanias 1.29.2.
89 Plutarch, Themistocles 22.1.

month being her sacred day). The condemned man was given wine to drink and then slain.[90]

This title is primarily linked to a temple built between the 6th and 5th century BCE in Athens by Themistocles, a non-aristocratic politician and military leader. On the Island of Rhodes, the name Aristiboule is used to refer to the Phrygian Mother Goddess.

## ASTRATEIA Αστρατεία

Pausanias[91] describes this title, meaning *stayed their advance*, referring to the shrine of Artemis at Pyrrhikhos, where the Amazons stayed their advance (i.e. stopped).

Pyrrhikhos was the name of one of the ten Curetes, a dancer. The Curetes were said to spring from the earth where the goddess Rhea grabbed the earth while giving birth to the baby, and went on to guard the baby and drum day and night to ensure that Kronos would not hear the baby's cries. The name is also used for a woodland god of the dance conflated with Silenus.

## ASTYRÍNÍ Αστυρήνη

This title, meaning *of Astyra*, refers to the worship of Artemis in the small town of Astyra in Troia, Anatolia[92], where there was a temple to this goddess. It was a place that had hot springs and was said to have a hot spring of black water.

## BASILEIS Βασιλεὶς

Herodotus[93] refers to Thracian and Paionian women sacrificing to Artemis *Basileis*, indicating *royalty or princess*.

---

90 Porphyry, De abstinentia.
91 Pausanias 3.25.3.
*92 Strabo 13.1.51 & 13.1.65.*
93 Herodotus 4.33.

## BRAURONIA Βραυρώνα

An eminent title for Artemis which simply means *of Brauron*, the location of one of her most popular temples.

Also see *Artemis of Brauron in Chapter 3*.

## COLAENIS Χολαινίς

In Aristophanes' play *The Birds*, Artemis is called Artemis *Colaenis*, meaning *of Colaenis*. An Athenian king who claimed to be a descendant of Hermes erected a temple to Artemis in this name at Myrrhinus.

## DAPHNAIÍ Δαφναία

A sanctuary to Artemis *Daphnaii*, meaning *of the laurel*, was situated in Hypsous in Lacedaemon.[94] Strabo mentions an annual festival to Artemis as *Daphnaii* and *Elaphiaia* at Olympia.[95]

## DEREATIS Ειλείθυια

An image of Artemis *Dereatis*, meaning *of Dereion*, was set up in the open at Dereion in Lacedaemon, next to a spring called Anonos.[96]

## EILEITHYIA Ειλείθυια

This title of *Eileithyia*, used in Orphic Hymn 2, meaning *helping goddess*, was given to Artemis as a divine midwife or birth goddess. It was also used for a group of unnamed divine attendants who assisted in childbirth as well as several other goddesses associated with childbirth, including Hekate and Hera.

---

94 Pausanias 3.24.9.
95 Strabo 8.3.12.
96 Pausanias 3.20.7.

Homer refers to the Eileithyiai as the daughters of Hera[97]. In the Orphic Hymn 2, which is to Prothyraia, Artemis *Eileithyia* is also named.

## ELAPHIAIA Ελαφιαία

Pausanias[98] mentions *Elaphiaia* as a title for Artemis, meaning *of the deer*. This is likely a reference to Artemis' role in the hunt and because she is frequently depicted as being accompanied by deer. Strabo also mentions an annual festival to Artemis *Elaphiaia* at Olympia.[99]

## ENODIA Εννοδία/ Ενοδία

A temple to Artemis *Enodia*, meaning *of the road*, was established at Pherai around 700 BCE. This title is more commonly associated with the goddess Hekate. Enodia may have originally been a separate goddess associated with roads and dog sacrifices.

## EPHESIA Εφέσια

A significant title of Artemis, meaning *of Ephesus*.

*See Artemis of Ephesus in Chapter 3.*

## EUKLEIA Ευκλεία

Pausanias wrote of a temple in Thebes to Artemis *Eukleia*, meaning *of fair fame* or *of good repute*, which had a stone lion statue in front of it. It was alleged that Herakles dedicated the temple after his victory over the Orkhomenians.[100]

Plutarch wrote some years before this, saying that though *Eukleia* was regarded as Artemis, some said she was the daughter of Herakles and Myrto, who died a virgin and was immortalised. She received divine honours from the Boiotians and Lokrians, with an

---

97 Iliad 11.270.
98 Pausanias 6.22.8.
99 Strabo 8.3.12.
100 Pausanias 9.17.1.

altar and image in every marketplace. As the Goddess of Good Repute, she was also given preliminary sacrifices by future brides and bridegrooms.[101]

Xenophon wrote of how a mixed band of Athenians, Argives and Boeotians attacked Thebes on the last day of the festival to Artemis *Eukleia* in 392 BCE to ensure they killed more people. The young Theban men drove them away.[102]

## EURYNOMI Ευρυνώμη

Pausanias[103] refers to Artemis by this title, meaning *the broad pasture*, concerning a shrine to her at Phigalia in Arcadia surrounded by cypress trees. In this form, Artemis was depicted as half woman and half fish, much like a mermaid, much like the depictions of the goddess Atagartis. The latter was worshipped along with the god Haddad in the area that is now Northern Syria.

## EUSTEPHANOS KELADEINE
Ευστέφανοσ Κελαδεινή

The Iliad describes Artemis as *Eustephanos Keladeine*, meaning *sweet-garlanded lady of clamours*, having its origins in a story where she complains to Zeus of having been hit by his wife, the goddess Hera.[104]

## HELEIA Ηελεία

Strabo gives this title, meaning *of the marsh*, for Artemis at her temple in the village of Helos in Southern Greece.[105]

## HEMERE Ημέρα

In Hymn 3 to Artemis, Callimachus refers to Artemis *Hemere*, meaning the gentle or she who soothes, as the aspect of a shrine at

---

101 Plutarch, Aristides 20.5.
102 Xenophon, The Hellenica.
103 Pausanias 8.41.4.
104 Iliad 21.470.
105 Strabo 8.3.25.

Lousa dedicated to her by Proitos for returning his daughters safely to him calmed of their wild spirits. Pausanias also refers to this shrine.[106]

# HIEREIA Ιερεια

A sanctuary at Oresthasion in Arcadia was dedicated to Artemis *Hiereia*, meaning priestesses.[107] There were three ways to become a priestess in Ancient Greece:

- Allotment
- Appointment
- Inheritance

Those who held such roles had some privileges, but it also came with the responsibility of being the temple's caretaker and fulfilling duties there.

# HÍGEMONÍ Ηγεμόνη

A sanctuary to Artemis *Hígemoní*, meaning *the leader*, was established in Sparta.[108] The hero, Khronios, set up a sanctuary for Artemis Hígemoní at Tegea, in Arcadia, after killing Aristomelidas, the despotic ruler of Orkhomenos. This was done at the instruction of the goddess Artemis after he caused a maiden to commit suicide.[109]

# HYMNIA Υμνία

Pausanias referred to a sanctuary of Artemis *Hymnia*, meaning *of hymns*, on the border of Orkhomenos in Arcadia and claimed that the Arcadians worshipped her there from the earliest times.[110] He also mentioned an annual festival held for her there[111]. He recorded that it was customary for the priests of Artemis *Hymnia* to live in

---

106 Pausanias 8.18.8.
107 Pausanias 8.44.2.
108 Pausanias 3.14.6, also 8.37.1.
109 Pausanias 8.47.6.
110 Pausanias 8.5.11.
111 Pausanias 8.13.1.

purity, abstaining from sex and washing and never entering private homes.[112]

## IOKHEAIRA Ιοχέαιρα AND HEKATEBOLON IOKHEAIRA Εκατηβόλον Ιοχέαιρα

Hesiod refers to Artemis with this title, meaning *delighter in arrows*, when describing her and Apollo as children of Zeus. It is also found in the Odyssey[113] and Homeric Hymn 3 to Apollo.[114]

The Homeric Hymn 9 names Artemis as *Hekatebolon Iokheaira*, a title meaning *far-shooting delighter in arrows*. Artemis is frequently depicted with a quiver of arrows, and arrows are frequently mentioned in Artemis' titles, showing how strongly they are associated with her. Again, this may be an example of the close connection between Hekate and Artemis.

## IPHIGENEIA Ιφιγένεια

There was a sanctuary at Hermione in Argolis of Artemis *Iphigeneia*, referring to the goddess/heroine who was a companion of Artemis, which may have been in honour of both.[115] As discussed previously, Iphigeneia was offered as a sacrifice to Artemis but rescued by the goddess at the last moment.

## ISSORIA Ισσωρία

Pausanias refers to a sanctuary of Artemis *Issoria*, meaning *of Issorion*, at Issorion in Sparta [116] and Teuthrone, both in Lacedaemon.[117]

---

112 Pausanias 8.13.1.
113 Odyssey 6.102.
114 Hesiod, Theogony 918.
115 Pausanias 2.35.1.
116 Pausanias 3.14.2 see also Plutarch's Lives Vol 2.
117 Pausanias 3.25.4.

## KALLISTE Καλλίστη

Kalliste, meaning *fairest* or *most beautiful*, is used as an epithet for her by Pausanias when he refers to the wooden image of Artemis found with the image of Artemis *Ariste*, in the precinct of Artemis in Athens.[118]

## KARYATIS Καρυάτις

At Karyai in Lacedaemon was an image of Artemis *Karyatis*, meaning *of the walnut trees*, where an image of Artemis was set out in the open. The area was sacred to Artemis and her Nymphs, and every year, the Lacedaemonn maidens would dance and sing chorally there.[119] The term *Caryatid*, for pillars shaped like female figures, is derived from the Greek Karyatides, the dancers of Artemis *Karyatis*.

## KEDREATIS Κεδρεάτις

This name, meaning *Lady of the Cedar*, refers to an image set in a cedar tree near the old city of Orkhomenos.[120]

## KHRYSELAKATOS Χρυσηλάκατος

This title frequently occurs in the Iliad[121] and Homeric Hymns (5 and 27). It means *with shafts of gold*, and refers to the golden arrows she uses to hunt and for inflicting disease if she became displeased, usually due to discourteous acts towards young women or herself.

## KHRYSAOROS Χρυσάωρ

Herodotus mentions this title, which means *golden-sworded* and refers to the headland of Kynosoura[122].

---

118 Pausanias 1.29.2, also 8.35.8.
119 Pausanias 3.10.7.
120 Pausanias 8.13.1.
121 Iliad 16.181.
122 Herodotus 8.77.

# KHRYSENIOS Χρυσήνιος

In the Iliad[123], Artemis is described by this title, meaning *the golden reins*, referring to her golden chariot. Four golden-horned deer drew this chariot.

# KHRYSOTHRONOS Χρυσόθρονος

The Odyssey[124] refers to Artemis by this title, meaning *golden-throned*, which also occurs in the Iliad[125].

# KINDYAS Κινδυάς

Strabo mentions a temple of Artemis *Kindyas*, meaning *of Kindye*, near Bargylia in Kos, where Kindye had been and where the rain was said to fall without ever hitting the temple.[126]

# KNAGIA Κναγία

Knageus was a Spartan hero who was taken prisoner in battle and sold as a slave to the Cretans. He lived in the sanctuary of Artemis but ran away with a maiden priestess, who took the image of Artemis with her. They subsequently set up a temple of Artemis *Knagia*, meaning *of Knageus*. This narrative corresponds closely to the story of Iphigeneia and Orestes.

# KNAKALÍSIA Κνακαλησία

This title, meaning *of Knakalos*, refers to the worship of Artemis at her sanctuary at Mount Knakalos in Arcadia.[127]

# KNAKEATIS Κνακεάτις

Pausanias mentions the ruins of a temple to Artemis *Knakeatis* near Tegea, above the modern village of Mavriki in the mountainous

---

123 Iliad 6.205.
124 Odyssey 5.119.
125 Iliad 9.530.
126 Strabo 14.2.20.
127 Pausanias 8.23.3

site known as Psili Korphi, in Arcadia.¹²⁸ The name might suggest a connection with wolves associated with Artemis, her brother Apollo, and their mother Leto.

## KOKKOKA Κοκκώκα

This name has several suggested meanings. It it might mean *of the pomegranate seed*.¹²⁹ Pausanias said he does not know why Artemis was given this surname.¹³⁰ It is also possible that this name links Artemis to κόκκος, the fruit of the Kermes Oak (*Quercus coccifera*). This is a food source for the Kermes scale insect harvested to create a deep red dye and in herbalism for pregnancy-related issues.

## KOLAINIS Κολαινίς

Callimachus records that Artemis had this name, meaning *hornless* because Agamemnon sacrificed a hornless ram made of wax for her. This resulted in her worship at Amarynthos in Euboia under this title.¹³¹ In the same fragment, Callimachus also wrote that the one-eyed and tailless were sacrificed to her.

## KOLOÍNÍS Κολοηνής

This title, meaning *of Koloe*, refers to Lake Koloe, formerly known as Lake Gygaia, near Sardis in Lydia. Strabo mentions that the baskets danced at the festivals celebrated here, denouncing this as 'talking of marvels' rather than the truth.¹³²

## KONDYLEATIS Κονδυλεάτις

Artemis was known by this title, meaning *of Kondylea*, a place near Kaphya. This was the location of the story of children putting a noose around the statue of the goddess' neck and then being stoned by the village's adults as punishment. The goddess demanded

---

128 Pausanias 8.53.11.
129 Sexual Culture in Ancient Greece – Garrison, 2000, p86.
130 Pausanias 5.15.7.
131 Callimachus Iambi Frag 6 (from Scholiast on Aristophanes The Birds 873).
132 Strabo 13.4.5.

reparation from the adults for their actions towards the children, and Artemis then became *Apankhomení (the strangled lady)* at this location.¹³³

## KORDAX Κόρδαξ

Artemis was well known for her connection with dancing, and this name associates her with the *Kordax*, a dance from Lydia sacred to her.¹³⁴

## KORE Κόρη

Callimachus refers to Artemis as *Kore* in Hymn 3 to Artemis, referring to the shrine set up by Proitos in her honour as Artemis *Kore* when she returned to him his maiden daughters who had been wandering the Azanian Hills. *Kore* means *maiden* and is a title given to other young virginal goddesses. It is most often associated with Persephone, Demeter's daughter before Hades takes her as his wife.

## KORYPHAIA Κορυφαία

A sanctuary was built at the top of Mount *Koryphon* in Argolis as *Koryphaia*, meaning *of the peak* or *summit*.¹³⁵

## KORYTHALIA Κορυθαλία

This name means *of the flowering of young branches*. It may refer either to the growth of vegetation or metaphorically to the development of children, as the *korythale* was *a laurel branch* carried ritually before marriage by young women and men.¹³⁶ Plutarch also states that one of Apollo's nurses was called *Korythaleia*, hinting at the role Artemis is sometimes given in Apollo's birth and her role as *kourotrophos*.¹³⁷

---

133 Pausanias 8.23.6.
134 Pausanias 6.22.1.
135 Pausanias 2.28.2.
136 See Choruses of Young Women in Ancient Greece – Calame, 1997, p170-71.
137 Plutarch, Moralia 657.

## LAPHRIA Λαφρία

Pausanias recounts this title, meaning *of Laphros*, being used after a Phocian hero called Laphros, who set up the image of Artemis at Calydon. After Emperor Augustus had laid waste to Calydon and the whole area of Aitolia around it, the statue of Artemis *Laphria* was given to the people of Patrai.[138] The festival of Laphria was celebrated annually in honour of Artemis at Patrai.

## LEUKOPHRUÍNÍ Λευκοφρυηνή

Pausanias tells how the Magnesians honoured Artemis as *Leukophruíní*, meaning *of the white bird*, dedicating a statue to her in this name in her temple in Magnesia[139] and erecting a bronze statue of her in this name in Athens.[140] Strabo wrote that although the Magnesian temple was inferior in size and quantity of votive offerings to Ephesus, the harmony and skill shown in its building were superior; he also notes it as the third largest temple in Asia after those of Artemis at Ephesus and Apollo at Didymoi (Didim).[141] All three of these temples are in relative proximity to each other.

## LIMNAIÍ Λιμναία

This title, meaning *Lady of the lake*, was used by Pausanias[142] to describe Artemis, but he tells us that it was a title of *Britomartis*. We have already seen examples of how Britomaris was subsumed into the figure and cult of Artemis. However, based on the number of references in his writings to other temples of Artemis *Limnaií* it seems to have been a commonly used title.[143]

## LOKHIA Λοχία

There was a sanctuary of Artemis *Lokhia*, meaning *helper in childbirth*, at her temple in Delos. Euripides refers to Artemis *Lokhia*

---

138 Pausanias 7.18.8.
139 Pausanias 3.18.7.
140 Pausanias 1.26.4, & 3.18.7.
*141 Strabo 14.1.40.*
142 Pausanias 3.14.2.
*143 See Pausanias 2.7.6, 3.23.10, 7.20.7, & 8.53.11.*

in two of his plays. In Iphigeneia in Tauris, Artemis *Lokhia* is described in a landscape of laurels, olive shoots and palm trees.[144] In *The Suppliants*, the mothers of children killed beneath the walls of Thebes weep because Artemis *Lokhia* no longer protects their children.[145]

# LYKEIÍ Λυκείη

According to Pausanias, *Lykeii*, meaning *of the wolves*, was a surname of Artemis among the Amazons, legendary female warriors thought to have originated near the Black Sea.[146]

# LYKOÍ Λυκόη

A bronze image of the goddess as Artemis *Lykoí*, meaning *of Lykoa*, was set in her temple at Lykoa in Arcadia, under Mount Mainalos.[147]

# MOUNYKHIA Μουνιχία

Pausanias refers to a temple of Artemis *Mounykhia*, meaning *of Mounykhia*, in the harbour of the port of the same name in Attica.[148] Strabo refers to the temple of Artemis *Mounykhia*, founded by Agamemnon in Pygela near Ephesus.[149] Suidas also mentions the sacrifice to Artemis *Mounykhia* in Athens during the month of Mounykhion.[150]

# MYSIA Μυσία

Pausanias records that on the road from Sparta to Arcadia was a sanctuary of Artemis *Mysia*, meaning *of Mysia*.[151]

---

144 Euripides, Iphigeneia in Tauris, 1097.
145 Euripides, Suppliants, 955.
146 Pausanias 2.31.4.
147 Pausanias 8.36.7.
148 Pausanias 1.1.4.
149 Strabo 14.1.20.
*150 Suidas, Mounykhion.*
151 Pausanias 3.20.9.

## NEMYDIA Νεμυδία

Strabo mentions a temple of Artemis *Nemydia* at the village of Teuthia in Elis.[152] It is not known what this name means.

## ORTHIA Ορθία

Pausanias refers to a sanctuary of Artemis on Mount Lykone, with marble images of her with her mother Leto and brother Apollo.[153] *Orthia* is taken to mean either *standing* or *of the steep*. It may have been the name of a Spartan goddess who became conflated with Artemis because they shared similar qualities and roles, such as fertility and childbirth.

## ORTHOSIA Ορθοσία

Herodotus mentions an altar of Artemis *Orthosia*, meaning *of Orthosia*, at the city of Byzantion on the Bosporus Strait.[154] Orthosia was a Carian city in Anatolia.

## PEITHO Πειθώ

A sanctuary at Argos was dedicated to Artemis *Peitho*, meaning *the persuasive*.[155]

## PERGAIA Περγαία

This title, meaning *of Perge*, was used at the temple near Perge in Pamphylia. A festival was celebrated there every year[156], according to Callimachus[157], with hymns composed by the poetess Damophyle in honour of Artemis *Pergaia*.[158]

---

152 Strabo 8.3.11.
153 Pausanias 2.24.5, see also 3.16.7.
154 Herodotus 4.87.
155 Pausanias 2.21.1.
156 Strabo 14.4.2.
157 Callimachus, Hymn 3 to Artemis.
*158 Life of Apollonius of Tyana 1.30.*

## PERSIA Περγαία

Artemis *Persia*, meaning *of Persia*, was celebrated at a sanctuary in Lydia.[159] The title *Persia* is also given to the goddess Hekate and may suggest origins or connections for both goddesses in that region.

## PHERAIA Φεραία

Although this title means *of the beasts*, Pausanias asserts that it originated from an image brought from Pherai in Thessalia.[160] In this region, Artemis was also worshipped as Enodia, the goddess of the roads. Enodia took the place of Artemis in the cult of the twelve gods and is also called the *Pheraian* goddess.

## PROPYLAIÍ Προπυλαία

According to Pausanias, the Eleusinians had a temple of Artemis *Propylaií*, meaning *of the gate*.[161] It is a title more often attributed to the goddess Hekate, whose shrines were placed explicitly at gateways and city entranceways.

## PROSEOIA Προσηώα

A small temple to Artemis *Proseoia* was located near the village of Hestiaia in Euboia. The name might mean *facing the East*, as this was an eastward-facing port.[162] Plutarch[163] wrote that this sanctuary was surrounded by a wall of marble, which turned the colour of saffron when it was rubbed.

---

159 Pausanias 7.6.6.
160 Pausanias 2.23.5, see also 2.10.7.
161 Pausanias 1.38.6.
*162 Plutarch, Themistocles 8.1.*
163 Life of Themistocles (VIII, 1)

## PROTOTHRONIÍ Πρωτοθρονία

Pausanias tells of an altar to Artemis *Protothronií*, meaning *of the first throne*, within a temple of Artemis *Ephesia* at Amphissa in Phocis.[164] An image of Nyx also stood in this temple.

## PYRONIA Πυρωνία

Pausanias describes a sanctuary to Artemis *Pyronia*, meaning *of the fire*, at Mount Krathis in Arcadia, where the people had used fire from the sanctuary of this fire goddess in their ceremonies.[165]

## RHOKKAIA Ροκκαία

This title, meaning *of Rhokkha*, refers to the worship of Artemis at the village of Rhokkha in Crete. Aelian described dogs in Rhokkha going mad and hurling themselves into the sea.[166] Aelian went on to say that boys bitten by these dogs were taken to the temple of Artemis for healing.[167]

## SARONIS Σαρωνίς

This title, meaning *of Saron*, refers to an Argosian hero, who established a sanctuary of Artemis near Troizenos in Argolis, where an annual festival called the Saronia was held.[168] He eventually died chasing a doe which swam into the sea. He followed the doe and drowned, and his body came ashore at the grove of Artemis by the Phoibaian lagoon, where it was buried within the sacred enclosure.[169]

---

164 Pausanias 10.38.6.
165 Pausanias 8.15.8.
166 Aelian, On Animals 12.22.
*167 Aelian, on Animals 14.20.*
168 Pausanias 2.32.10.
169 Pausanias 2.30.7.

## SARPEDONIA Σαρπηδόνια

At Pylai in Kilikia (Anatolia) was the temple and oracle of Artemis *Sarpedonia*, meaning *of Sarpedon*,[170] a Lycian hero who may have established the temple.

FIGURE 13 ARTEMIS, LIMESTONE FIGURINE, CIRCA 300 BCE FROM THE SANCTUARY AT PYLAI.

## SELASPHOROS Σελασφόρος

Pausanias refers to altars to Artemis *Selasphoros*, meaning *the light carrier*, in the Attic towns of Phyla and Myrrhinos.[171]

## SKIATIS Σκιάτις

Pausanias refers to a sanctuary of Artemis *Skiatis*, meaning *of Skias*, which was said to have been built by the tyrant Aristodemos at Skias near Megalopolis in Arcadia.[172]

---

170 Strabo 14.5.19.
171 Pausanias 1.31.4.
172 Pausanias 8.35.5.

## SKYTHIA Σκυθία

This title, meaning *of Scythia*, is referred to in the Life of Apollonius of Tyana. In response to questions from the Egyptian sage Thespesion, Apollonius describes the ritual scourging done in honour of Artemis *Skythia*. The scourging would continue until blood flowed freely, and the blood from the wounds would be smeared on the altar, as prescribed by the oracle.

When asked why the Greeks did not sacrifice people as the Skythoi previously did, Apollonius replied that the Greeks should not adopt in full the manners and customs of barbarians.[173]

## SOTEIRA Σώτειρα

This title, meaning *saviour*, is often used for Artemis, where she played a role in safeguarding. Pausanias recounts how the Megarans (people of Megara) named Artemis *Soteira* after she helped them against the army of General Mardonios, making a bronze image in her honour.[174] An identical bronze image was installed at a temple at Pagai in Megara.[175] Pausanias also mentions Theseus starting a temple to Artemis *Soteira* when he returned to Troizenos in Argolis after defeating the Minotaur.[176]

The city of Boiai in Lacedaemon had a shrine to Artemis *Soteira* after her help revealed the site where the city should be built.[177] Processions for Artemis were begun from the sanctuary of Artemis *Soteira* by the people of Phigalia in Arcadia.[178]

The epithet *Soteira* was regularly used for the goddesses Hekate and Athena. All three of these are virgin goddesses, which might indicate that these goddesses are incorruptible, independent, and able to defend themselves, as they did not need the support of a male partner. For these reasons, they could fulfil the role of soteira effectively and fairly.

---

173 *Life of Apollonius of Tyana* 6.20.
174 Pausanias 1.40.2.
175 Pausanias 1.44.4.
176 Pausanias 2.31.4.
177 Pausanias 3.22.12. Other references include 7.27.4, & 8.30.10.
178 Pausanias 8.39.5.

# STYMPHALIA Στυμφαλία

This title, meaning *of Stymphalos*, refers to Stymphalos, in Arcadia, famed for the Stymphalian birds. Pausanias went into some detail about the sanctuary here, mentioning carvings of the Stymphalian birds near the temple's roof. He also describes white marble statues of maidens with bird legs standing behind the temple, known as Stymphalian Nymphs.

Pausanias believed that the celebrations and rites of the festival of Artemis *Stymphalia* were celebrated carelessly. He recorded that a log fell into the mouth of the chasm through which the river descended, preventing drainage, flooding the plain and creating the marshes. Later, when a hunter chased a deer into the marsh, the hunter and the hunted were swallowed up by the chasm. The river followed them, drying out the entire plain. Worshippers at Stymphalos subsequently paid far more respect and made a more considerable effort to honour Artemis properly.[179]

# TAURIA Ταυρία AND
# TAUROPOLOS Ταυροπόλος

Both these titles can be translated as *of Tauros*. Pausanias refers to the old wooden image of Artemis in Brauron as Artemis *Tauria*.[180] Strabo refers to Artemis *Tauropolos*, in Skythia, saying that Orestes and Iphigeneia took the rites from there to Komana in Cappadocia (Asia Minor, modern Türkiye), where she was identified with a Cappadocian goddess.[181] Cassius Dio refers to the statue of Tauric Artemis at Cappadocia and her worship there, giving a date of 68 BCE.

The Cappadocian goddess may have been the goddess Ma, who was both a Moon and Warrior goddess worshipped alongside the god Mēn; this goddess is also equated to goddesses such as Enyo, Hekate, Bellona and Kybele.

---

[179] Pausanias 8.22.7.
[180] Pausanias 1.23.7.
[181] Strabo 12.2.3.

## TRIKLARIA Τρικλαρία

*Triklaria*, meaning *of the three settlements*, refers to the communal worship of Artemis by the people of three settlements.[182] The temple of Artemis *Triklaria* at Patrai was defiled by the love-making of Lomaitho and Melanippos in the temple's inner sanctuary (see the section on Lomaitho and Melanippos).

## BROMIA Βρομία

This epithet, meaning *noisy one* or *thunderer*, is found in Orphic Hymn 36. It is the female equivalent of Bromios, a title of Dionysus, and emphasises the link between these two deities, both of whom had an ecstatic aspect.

## CYNTHIA Κυνθία

Ovid refers to Artemis by the name of *Cynthia* in his Fasti.[183] It is derived from *Mount Cynthus* on the island of Delos, where Artemis was said to have been born. Athena was sometimes also referred to as Athena Cynthia after her shrine on the same mountain. The epithet is shared with the goddess Diana, whose cult became equated with that of Artemis and other deities during the Roman period.

## DELIA Δελία

Another epithet used by Ovid, meaning *of Delos*, the island of her birth.[184]

## DIKTYNNA Δίκτυννα

Orphic Hymn 36 and Aristophanes both refer to Artemis as *Diktynna*[185], meaning *of the hunting nets*, which is also the name of the Cretan goddess who was subsumed into the worship of Artemis and subsequently portrayed as one of her hunting companions.

---

182 Pausanias 7.19.1 and 7.22.11.
183 Ovid, Fasti 2.155, and Metamorphoses 2.414, 7.732.
184 Ovid Fasti 5.493.
185 Aristophanes, Frogs 1358.

Callimachus describes this in his Hymn 3 to Artemis, referring to her as *Diktynna* named after the Cretan nymph. Pausanias refers to an annual festival of Artemis *Diktynna* at her temple in Hypsous in Lacedaemon.[186] The goddess Hekate was likewise equated to Diktynna.

We are told that *Diktynna* was sexually pursued by King Minos, who was in lust with her. She fled from him and eventually threw herself into the sea to escape the King. She was rescued by fishermen and taken to the island of Aegina (near mainland Greece), where she continued to be worshipped, perhaps as the goddess Aphaia.

In one version of the story of *Diktynna's* arrival on Aegina, we are told that Artemis had turned the nymph into Hekate. Hekate, *Diktynna* and Aphaia are all conflated and all of them are depicted with dogs.

## ELAPHABOLOS Ελαφηβόλοσ

From Homeric Hymn 27, this title means *deer-shooting*, and refers to her role as supreme huntress, and deer, her favourite prey.

## HEKAERGE Εκαέργη

This title of Artemis, meaning *far working*, is also the name of one of her attendants. Callimachus refers to Hekaerge in one place as Artemis,[187] and in another as one of the daughters of Boreas (the North Wind).[188]

## HEURIPPA Ευρίππη

This name, meaning *horse-finder*, was said to come from Odysseus, who set up a sanctuary for Artemis at *Pheneos* in Arcadia after finding his lost mares there.[189]

---

186 Pausanias 3.24.9, see also 10.36.5.
187 Callimachus, Hymn 4 to Delos.
188 Callimachus, Hymn 4 to Delos.
189 Pausanias 8.14.5.

## IOKHEAIRA Ἰοχέαιρα

From Homeric Hymn 27 this title means *delighter in arrows*. This is an obvious reference to Artemis' skill in archery and this title were frequently combined with other epithets, such as *Hekatebolon Iokheaira* and *Theroskopos Iokheaira*.

## KELADEINE Κελαδεινή

In the Iliad[190] and Homeric Hymn 27 this epithet is used for Artemis. It means *strong-voiced* and refers to Artemis as a singer, emphasizing her musical ability.

## KHITONE Χιτώνη

Found in Callimachus Hymn 3 to Artemis, this title means *of the tunic* and refers to the short hunting tunic worn by Artemis, known as a khitone.

## KOUROTROPHOS Κουροτρόφοσ

This title, meaning *child's nurse*, was sometimes used for Artemis as well as for the goddesses Hekate, Hera and Gaia.

## LIMENOSKOPE Λιμνεσκόπη

Callimachus Hymn 3 to Artemis describes her as *Limenoskope*, meaning *watcher of harbours*, referring to her role as guardian of harbours previously mentioned in the same hymn.

## LÍTOIS Λητώις

This name, meaning *daughter of Leto*, is found in Ovid.[191]

---

190 Iliad 16.181.
191 Ovid, Metamorphoses 7.384.

## LYGODESMÍ Λυγοδέσμαν

This title was given to the statue found by Astrabakos and Alopekos, and installed in the shrine at Ortygia. It means *willow-bound*, a reference to the icon being found in a thicket of willow.[192]

## ORSILOKHIA Ορσιλοχία

This translates as *helper in childbirth*. Antoninus Liberalis refers to this title as being the name given to Iphigeneia when she became the immortal companion of Akhilleus (Achilles).[193]

## PAIDOTROPHOS Παιδοτρόφος

There was a temple to Artemis as *Paidotrophos*, meaning *child nurse*, at Korone in Messenia.[194]

## PARTHENON AIDOINE Παρθένον Αιδοίην

From Homeric Hymn 27, this title, meaning *revered virgin*, emphasises Artemis's virginal nature.

## PARTHENOS Παρθένος

Artemis was referred to by Callimachus as *Parthenos*, meaning *virgin*.[195] There was a temple of Artemis *Parthenos* on the island of Leros.

## PHOEBE Φοίβη

This title, meaning *light*, was used by Ovid [196] and Aristophanes[197] and also emphasised the link with her twin brother Apollo, known as Phoebus, the male form of light.

---

192 Pausanias 3.16.7.
193 Antoninus Liberalis, Metamorphoses, 27.
194 Pausanias 4.34.6.
195 Callimachus, Hymn 3 to Artemis.
196 Ovid, Metamorphoses 2.414, and Fasti 2.155.
197 Aristophanes, Lysistrata.

The Titan goddess Phoebe, the mother of Asteria and Leto, was the grandmother of Artemis and Apollo. The Titan Phoebe was the goddess of the Delphic Oracle after Gaia, it was then occupied by the Python, which Apollo killed before taking on the role of the god at this important temple.

## PHOSPHORUS Φώσφορος

The title, meaning *light-bringer*, is found in Callimachus Hymn 3 to Artemis, where she demands the title from Zeus. It is a title she shared with Hekate, who is more often associated with it. Pausanias also refers to a statue of Artemis Phosphorus in the sanctuary of Asclepius in Messene.[198] As Phosphorus, she would have been depicted with one or two torches and may have been associated with the Moon or Venus, bringing light to the dark.

## POTNA THEA Πότνα\Πότνια Θεά

Artemis is mentioned in the Odyssey as *Potna Thea*, meaning *goddess queen*.[199]

## POTNIA THERON Πότνια Θηρῶν

Artemis is described in the Iliad as *Potnia Theron*, meaning *Queen of wild beasts*. This title suggests both her role as Lady of the Animals and her favoured hunting activity. It is an ancient title of the nameless Minoan Lady of the Beasts, which Artemis later assumed. Potnia is a Mycenaean word adopted by the ancient Greeks and can be translated as Lady, Mistress or Queen. Regardless of what the Minoans may have called her, it is interesting to note that a similar goddess was worshipped throughout the Aegean basin and the ancient Near East, which may provide further clues to her origins.

---

[198] Pausanias 4.31.10.
[199] Odyssey 20.60.

## THEROSKOPOS IOKHEAIRA
Θηροσκόποσ Ιοχέαιρα

The meaning of this title from Homeric Hymn 27, *the huntress who delights in arrows*, is self-explanatory.

## TITYOKTONE Τιτυοκτόνε

This title, meaning *slayer of Tityos*, refers to Artemis killing the giant of this name when he tried to molest her mother Leto.[200]

FIGURE 14: DETAIL OF THE 16TH CENTURY COPY OF ARTEMIS OF EPHESUS, IN THE GARDEN OF VILLA D'ESTE, TIVOLI (ITALY, NEAR ROME). IN THIS ICONIC FOUNTAIN, WATER RUNS FROM ARTEMIS' BODY.

---

200 Callimachus, Hymn 3 to Artemis.

# 7.
# A VIRGIN GODDESS

*Wonder what young intruder dares to sing*
*In these still haunts, where never foot of man*
*Should tread at evening, lest he chance to spy*
*The marble limbs of Artemis and all her company*
- Oscar Wilde, The Garden of Eros, 1881-

Artemis declared as a child that she would remain forever *parthenos*, i.e. a virgin. In Callimachus' Hymn to Artemis, the young goddess sits on his knee and requests of her father, *"Give me to keep my maidenhood, Father, forever: and give me to be of many names, that Phoebus may not vie with me.[201]"*

This is reflected in descriptions of her and several epithets given to Artemis:

- *Hagní Parthenos*, the pure virgin
- *Aidoios Parthenos*, the revered virgin
- *Parthenos Iokheaira*, the virgin who delights in arrows.

Artemis' virginity is a significant part of her character, and she prized the virginity of her attendants, which was illustrated by the severe punishments she effected on those who lost their virginity, regardless of the cause, even when it was rape by a god. This demonstrates that the virginity referred to as it relates to Artemis was a complete absence of sexual activity.

## WHAT'S A VIRGIN?

This is not as straightforward a question as it might seem. There are a lot of different interpretations of what virginity might have meant or referred to in the ancient world compared to the definitions in use today.

---

201 Callimachus, Hymn to Artemis (circa 300BCE). Trans. Mair, 1921.

*Parthenos*, the word most often translated from Greek into English as *virgin*, can be understood to mean a girl still living under her father's or family's protection and who has never had sexual intercourse – at least, this was the ideal situation.

Those from less privileged families had to work in circumstances without the same level of protection, and many would have had intercourse by choice and sometimes by force before marriage. If the sexual union remained undiscovered and there were no consequences (such as pregnancy), the girls could and would go on claiming virginity. Sometimes, even if a child were born, the birth would be considered a *virgin birth*, and the mother could continue to claim virginity. Virgin births were often associated with claims that provided a child with a special status – as the child of a god, even if the woman had a husband.

The term *Parthenos* referred both to young ladies who had never had sexual intercourse, as well as those who did but successfully managed to hide it from their communities. However, for the goddess Artemis, covering up sexual intercourse by pretending it didn't happen didn't hold, as illustrated by examples where her attendants could not defend themselves from the advances of a suitor or willingly gave themselves to a man.

In the ancient world, virginity, with no previous sexual intercourse, was definitely the ideal – not only was it revered by some, but it also provided the one sure method of ensuring that the children a woman birthed would be attributed to the husband, thereby ensuring inheritance and the continuation of a bloodline. Again, this would have been more important to those who held higher societal positions and those who owned property. While effective birth control and DNA testing have changed a lot of things for us today, virginity and sexual innocence remain valued in some societies and cultures, and where this is the case, women continue to cover up previous sexual encounters where they can. The rights or wrongs of all aspects of this is a subject of much debate.

# VIRGINITY MEANT POWER

Very few goddesses hold the status of *parthenos*, and when they do, it is never a sign of weakness but rather the opposite: power.

Being a Virgin Goddess indicated that the goddess could defend herself or that they had protection from a powerful male deity – or both. At no point did it mean weakness or subjugation, as some associate with the Virgin Mary of the Roman Catholic Church, who, albeit differently, also holds great power to this day.

Artemis was an effective warrior and huntress, and she also enjoyed the protection of her father Zeus. [202] Athena was an impressive warrior and could defend herself. Hestia rejected the advances of powerful gods and received the protection of Zeus, enabling her to remain a virgin forever. Hekate was a formidable goddess who protected homes, temples and cities and proved herself a warrior.

The Virgin Goddesses had a special status because of their virginity, which set them aside as independent, strong and commanding. These virgin goddesses had immunity from the wiles of Aphrodite. Homer tells us that laughter-loving Aphrodite could never tame Artemis in love, saying that the huntress loved archery and slaying wild beasts in the mountains, writing that:

> *"Nor does laughter-loving Aphrodite ever tame in love*
> *Artemis, the huntress with shafts of gold; for she loves*
> *archery and the slaying of wild beasts in the mountains,*
> *the lyre also and dancing and thrilling cries*
> *and shady woods and the cities of upright men."* [203]

Eros could also not affect Artemis with his arrows of love. Sappho went as far as to say that Eros never approached Artemis.[204]

Aristophanes also stressed the chastity of Artemis in his play Woman at the Thesmophoria:

> *Agathon:*
> *And praise Artemis too, the maiden huntress,*
> *who wanders on the mountains and through the woods.*

---

202 See Callimachus, Hymn 3.
203 Homeric Hymn 5 to Aphrodite, 6.
204 Greek Lyric I Sappho Frag 34.

*Agathon's Chorus:*
*I, in my turn, celebrate the everlasting happiness of the chaste Artemis, the mighty daughter of Leto!*[205]

Euripides likewise emphasised this point, going as far as calling her *"most virginal"*.[206]

The concept of virginity associated with Artemis is best understood in the sense of a female who has not had sexual intercourse. Her nymphs are not all referred to as parthenos, so we can't say that that was a requirement, but based on extant mythology, it does appear that they were expected to be celibate while in the retinue of Artemis.

Following are a few examples of stories involving sexual advances and intercourse specifically linked to Artemis. As a sworn virgin and an effective warrior, it was dangerous for gods and mortals to attempt to force their adorations onto Artemis and her attendants. Even inappropriately looking at Artemis often had devastating consequences. Notwithstanding, many mortals and gods ignored the stories driven by their love and lust.

# ALPHEIOS

Alpheios, a river god, fell in love with Artemis and decided to try his 'luck' with her at an all-night gathering she held with her nymphs. Artemis suspected Alpheios would try this, so she smeared her face with mud and made all the other nymphs do likewise. Frustrated at being unable to recognize Artemis, Alpheios gave up and left.[207] While Alpheios failed to woo the Goddess of the Hunt, he was lucky compared to others who tried, and he managed to get away with his life intact. He later turned his attention to the nymph Arethousa.

---

205 Women at the Thesmophoria, Aristophanes, Trans. O'Neill.
206 Euripides, Hippolytus.
207 Pausanias 6.22.8.

## PROTECTING THE NYMPHS

As well as punishing those of her companions who lost their virginity, Artemis did her best to protect those threatened. In one example, she turned the Arcadian nymph Arethousa into a spring, Syrinx into a river and Amethyst into a rock to save them.

## HIPPOLYTUS & REX NEMORENSIS

When the young prince Hippolytus, who devoted his chaste life to Artemis, was killed through the machinations of Aphrodite, Artemis persuaded the god of healing, Asclepius, to bring Hippolytus back to life. The resurrected Hippolytus becomes her temple attendant at the temple of Diana at Lake Nemi temple, Aricia (Italy), where Artemis' myths and worship became conflated with that of Diana.

15 - COIN SHOWING DIANA NEMORENSIS:
SAID TO BE THE GODDESSES DIANA, HEKATE AND SELENE.

He may have been the first *Rex Nemorensus* (King of the Woods, a guardian role) at this famous temple, perhaps acting as guardian of the temple. Diana of Nemi was considered the huntress with bow and arrows and the goddess of three forms and roads. She is named *Trivia (of the three ways)* in her triple form and is designated as a combination of the goddesses Artemis, Hekate, and Selene. The goddess Hekate is also depicted in single and triple form and has the Greek epithet *Trioditis*, which, like the Roman *Trivia*, refers to the three ways or three roads.

At this volcanic lake, also known as *Speculum Dianae* or *The Mirror of Diana* by the poet Virgil, an uninterrupted veneration of the goddess continued for at least a millennium. The illustrious figure of the *Rex Nemorensis*, or *King of the Woods*, assumed dual roles as the high priest and custodian of the temple dedicated to Diana at this sacred site. Central to the religious observance was the celebrated Nemoralia, an eminent festival in honour of Diana, which originated at Lake Nemi and lasted for three days during the full moon period in August. This festival was also known as the Hecatean Ides.

## SACRED PROSTITUTION

There is no evidence to support the spurious claims that the temple of Artemis of Ephesus practised sacred prostitution or for its inclusion in the cult of Artemis elsewhere. None of the classical writers hints at such a thing, and none of the numerous inscriptions from and about Ephesus suggest that sacred prostitution ever occurred here. Our evidence for practices and beliefs linked to sexuality at this temple indicates the opposite.

Naturally, there is evidence of prostitution in the city of Ephesus. It was a large port city, so it is hardly a surprise to find that sexual services were offered for money. However, just because it happened in the city, does not connect it to the temple or worship of Artemis in Ephesus.

When we consider the myths associated with the Ephesian Artemis and her temple, along with other goddesses linked to the temple and the priestesses who served there, there is a consistent emphasis on their virginity. The priestesses mentioned serving at Ephesus are listed as *daughter of* rather than *wife of* when their names are provided, indicating their unmarried status. This, in turn, suggests that those who served Artemis at this temple held an unmarried and, accordingly, virginal status.

# 8.
# GODDESS OF WOMEN

Although most Greek goddesses had some link with childbirth, Artemis was particularly associated with the role of divine midwife protecting both mother and child during this challenging transition. According to Apollodorus[208], this is a role she stepped into as a newborn deity, assisting her mother, Leto, with the birth of her twin brother Apollo, though she was only born the day before herself.

## THE YOUNG

Artemis and Apollo are both protectors of young children. Hesiod recorded that they had assistance in this role:

- Artemis by the Sea Nymphs called Oceanides (Clouds) to look after girls.
- Apollo by the Potamoi (Rivers) to look after the boys.

However, Artemis alone was regarded as the protector of children from birth through to weaning, as Kourotrophos, and Paidotrophos. She also held the role of protector of infant animals.

A girl would be under the protection of Artemis until her consecration into womanhood. Girls were rededicated to Hera (the goddess of marriage) or Aphrodite (the goddess of love) when they reached maturity. The young girls made offerings to Artemis, honouring and thanking her for caring for them and leaving their childhood behind. At some coming-of-age ceremonies, girls would dedicate a lock of their hair to Artemis for the same reason.[209] It has been suggested that the hairlock symbolised the childhood the girl was leaving behind.[210]

Similar hair-cutting rituals also existed for boys during some rites of puberty.

---

208 Apollodorus 1.21.
209 See e.g. Apollodorus 6.276, Pausanias 1.43.4.
210 See e.g. Sacred Marriage in the Rituals of Greek Religion - Aphrodite Avagianou, 1991, 3 , and Marriage to Death: The Conflation of Wedding and Funeral Rituals in Greek Tragedy - Rush Rehm, 1994.

# CHILDBIRTH

Artemis was particularly associated with birth as the protectress of newborn children, as *Orsilokhia*, which means *helper of childbirth*. She was invoked as Artemis Orsilokhia during labour to protect the infant child. Women believed that Artemis could give them an easy birth at the full moon when animals were also observed to have an easier labour.[211] In his Hymn 3 to Artemis[212], Callimachus suggests that Leto had a trouble and pain-free time when she gave birth to Artemis. It is one of the reasons why Artemis was petitioned for help in childbirth.

# EILEITHYIA

Artemis shared the title of *Eileithyia*, or *helping goddess*, with several other goddesses and divine midwives. Although this title was strongly associated with Artemis, the Greek writer Homer named Eileithyia the goddess of birth-pain. He also wrote about many other *Eileithyiai*, whom he called the daughters of Hera. Hesiod also suggested that Eileithyia was the daughter of Zeus and Hera; or that she was the goddess Hekate.

It is worth noting that there was a well-established cult of the goddess Eileithyia in Crete, centred around the locations of Lato and Eleutherna. Offerings found in caves at Amnisos and Inatos demonstrate that she was a popular deity who flourished throughout the Hellenistic and Roman periods. Eileithyia in Crete may have had a unique role in raising Zeus after Rhea tricked Kronos into swallowing a rock rather than the newborn deity. This myth is at odds with the idea that Zeus is Artemis' father, but of course, the mythologies of the gods are not necessarily chronological or fixed. The goddess Hekate is depicted on a frieze at her late Hellenistic temple at Lagina, Türkiye, as nursing Zeus. This region's people may originally have been tribes who lived on boats around the island of Crete. If true, they likely brought some of their gods and religious practices. Votive offerings to Artemis Kourotrophos have been

---

211 Greek Lyric I Alcaeus Frag 390 (from Scholiast on Iliad).
212 Callimachus, Hymn 3 to Artemis.

found at Orthia. These were made of ivory and depicted Artemis, sometimes with attendant birth goddesses (Eileithyiai).

# AURA

Artemis delivered the babies of the Titan goddess Aura. She did this even though she was angry at her for being verbally abusive and becoming pregnant after her rape by Dionysus. Artemis may have been more forgiving if Aura had not immediately eaten one of her newborn babies.[213]

# IPHIGENEIA

Iphigeneia is described as receiving the clothes of women who died in childbirth.[214] This might be because Iphigeneia is defined variously, as an aspect of Artemis, as a companion or priestess to Artemis, or a mortal girl who was turned into the goddess Hekate by Artemis.

By the 7th century BCE Iphigeneia had become a companion of Artemis. She was the daughter of King Agamemnon, who had angered Artemis by killing a deer and then boasting he was a better hunter than her. Artemis calmed the wind to prevent his fleet from leaving for Troy, and to appease her Agamemnon was advised to sacrifice his daughter Iphigeneia by a soothsayer. He did so, but at the last moment, Artemis took pity and substituted a deer in her place, taking Iphigeneia as one of her companions.[215]

---

213 Dionysiaca 48.848.
214 Euripides, Iphigeneia in Tauris, see also The Temple Legends of Arkteia – William Sale, in Rheinisches Museum für Philologie Volume 1:265-84, 1975.
215 Proclus, Chrestomathia.

# 9.
# LADY OF THE HUNT & WILD ANIMALS

*"Praise Artemis also, the maiden huntress,
she who wanders on the mountains and through the
woods."* [216]

Artemis is the goddess of the hunt, whose favourite pursuit is exercising her skill as a huntress. She is Theroskopos (*hunter of wild beasts*) and Khitone (*goddess who wears the short hunting tunic*). The Eleans, people from Elis in southern Greece on the Peloponnese, were thought to call her Artemis Elaphiaia after her pursuit of hunting deer [*elaphos*][217], highlighting her passion for the hunt. This theme occurs repeatedly, such as in the Orphic Hymns, where she is described as the foe of the stag.[218]

Artemis was extremely good at getting what she wanted from her father Zeus. As a child, she asked him to give her arrows and a bow to slay wild animals and the mountains to hunt and dwell on.[219]

Many of her titles refer to her skill with her bow, the main instrument of the hunt. She is Artemis Iokheaira [*delighting in arrows*] and Theroskopos Iokheaira [*the huntress who delights in arrows*], roaming the mountains and taking her pleasure in hunting boars and running deer.[220]

*"Artemis Khryselakatos loves archery and
the slaying of wild beasts in the mountains."*[221]

Callimachus made frequent reference to Artemis' skill with the bow in his hymns to her: *"whose study is the bow and the shooting of hares*

---

216 Aristophanes, Thesmophoriazusae 114.
217 Pausanias 6.22.8.
218 Orphic Hymn 36 to Artemis.
219 Callimachus, Hymn 3 to Artemis.
220 Odyssey 6:102.
221 Homeric Hymn 5 to Aphrodite.

*and the spacious dance and sport upon the mountains."*, and again when he wrote, *"And how often goddess, did you make trial of thy silver bow?"*[222]

Many of the depictions of Artemis with animals show her holding one in each hand, either by their neck or hind-paws. This is the sort of position we would associate with carrying game and may indicate her role as goddess of the hunt rather than as goddess of animals.

## THE HUNTRESS

*"[Artemis] draws her golden bow ...*
*The tops of the high mountains tremble ...*
*and the sea also where fishes shoal."* [223]

Artemis was extremely proud of her hunting ability and confident in her supremacy, as would be expected for a goddess who was the patron of hunting.[224] When King Agamemnon boasted he was a better hunter than Artemis, the goddess prevented the Greek fleet from sailing for Troy. Only by offering his daughter as a sacrifice did Agamemnon appease Artemis, who snatched her up and substituted a deer as the killing blow was made, as discussed previously.

Another hunter, Broteas, son of King Tantalus (brother of Niobe), did not honour Artemis. He boasted of his ability, so Artemis made him kill himself by burning himself to death.[225] As mentioned, in some versions of the tale, Artemis killed the giant Orion for his hubris when he claimed to be better at hunting than her.

Artemis was a goddess of the hunt and also of the wild animals that she hunted. She demonstrated conservation principles by protecting young animals ensuring the species' propagation. References were frequently made to Artemis regarding this role. Consequently, she is Artemis sovereign of all creatures,[226] Artemis

---

222 Callimachus, Hymn 3 to Artemis.
223 Homeric Hymn 27 to Artemis.
224 Xenophon, Cynegeticus, 1.
225 Apollodorus E2.2.
226 Dionysiaca 11:344.

Agrotera [of the wilderness], and Potnia Theron [Lady of wild beasts].[227]

In his manual for hunters, Xenophon describes the prayer the hunter spoke as he released the hunting hounds:

*"To thee thy share of this chase, Lord Apollo; and thine to thee, O Huntress Queen!"*[228]

In addition to protecting young animals, Artemis also protects their mothers, and hunting female animals could have fatal consequences. On one occasion, a hunter called Saron of Troizenos chased a doe when it swam into the sea. He drowned, and his body washed up at the grove of Artemis at the Phoibaian lagoon.[229] Even Saron's earlier good deeds in setting up a temple to Artemis counted for nothing when he broke this hunting taboo.

It was said that wild animals would behave as if they were tame within the boundaries of the temple of Artemis, recognizing its powers of sanctuary. Strabo records this, describing how deer herded with wolves and allowed people to stroke them.[230]

Additionally, animals would find their way to her sacred places to give birth to their young, recognising this quality of sacred protection from the mistress of the animals.[231]

Those who had killed animals and were uncertain about the goddess' favour were wise to propitiate her quickly rather than risk her wrath. Hippolytus and Alkathoos are described as building temples to Artemis after slaying wild beasts.[232]

Sometimes, choosing one goddess in preference to another had consequences, as the maiden Polyphonte found out. This princess of the Triballoi tribe of Thrace was a hunting companion of Artemis, having scorned love and Aphrodite.

---

227 Iliad 21:470.
228 Xenophon, Cynegeticus, 20.
229 Pausanias 2.30.7.
230 Strabo 5.1.9.
231 Strabo 14.1.29.
232 Pausanias 2.31.4.

In revenge, Aphrodite makes Polyphonte go mad and make love with a bear. Artemis was disgusted by this and turned the other animals against her, killing her.[233]

## ARTEMIS & ANIMALS

Some animals were considered particularly sacred to Artemis. Chief amongst these were the deer, the dog and the bear, but they also included the boar, the hare and possibly the lion. Several birds were considered sacred to her, including the partridge, quail and buzzard.

## ARTEMIS & BEARS

The bear was especially sacred to Artemis as the creature and as the stellar constellation of Ursa Major, the Great Bear. Killing her sacred bears was the surest way of bringing down Artemis' wrath, as the Athenians found out on at least two occasions.

When the Athenians killed a female bear that appeared at the shrine of Artemis at Mounykhia (Attica), the goddess punished the locals with famine.[234]

On another occasion, a tame she-bear that played with the virgins at the sanctuary at Brauron scratched one of the girls after being provoked. The girl's brothers speared the she-bear and killed it, angering Artemis, who sent a pestilential sickness upon the Athenians. When the Athenians consulted an oracle, they were told the girls would hereafter have to play the part of the she-bear in the rites performed at Brauron as the blood price to atone for killing the bear.[235] As her cult animal, the bear was primarily celebrated in the rites of Artemis. Young girls aged between five and fifteen (scholars seem to disagree on the exact age) partook in rites where they dressed in saffron robes and acted as bears.

---

233 Antoninus Liberalis, Metamorphoses, 21.
234 Suidas, Embaros eimi.
235 Suidas, Arktos e Brauroniois.

> *"The Athenians decreed that no virgin might be given in marriage to a man if she hadn't previously played the bear for the goddess."*[236]

A charm from the Greek Magical Papyri called on Artemis as the Great Bear to assist the magician in achieving their goal, whatever that may be.

> *"Bear, Bear, you who rule the heaven, the stars, and the whole world; you who make the axis turn and control the whole cosmic system by force and compulsion;*
>
> *I appeal to you, imploring and supplicating that you may do the NN thing, because I call upon you with your holy names at which your deity rejoices, names which you are not able to ignore: Brimō, earth-breaker, chief huntress, Baubo Aumōr Amōr Amōr Iēa [shooter] of deer Amam Aphrou Ma, universal queen, queen of wishes, Amama, well-bedded, Dardanian, all-seeing, night-running, man-attacker, man-subduer, man-summoner, man-conqueror, Lichrissa Phaessa, O aerial one, O strong one, O song and dance, guard, spy, delight, delicate, protector, adamant, adamantine, O Damnameneia, Brexerikandara, most high, taurian, unutterable, fire-bodied, light-giving, sharply armed. Do such and such things."*[237]

# ARTEMIS & BIRDS

Ground-dwelling birds that could be hunted were particularly popular with Artemis, though other birds also feature in the myths about her. This section explores examples of some interactions between Artemis and birds.

## Partridges

Aelian recording tells us that the partridge (perdix) was the darling of Artemis[238].

---

236 Suidas, Arktos e Brauroniois.
237 PGM VII:686-702.
238 Aelian, On Animals 10.35.

## Artemis & Quails

The quail (ortyx) was sacred to both Artemis and her mother Leto. The island of Artemis' birth, Delos, was previously named Ortygia after the quail and linked to a story of the star goddess Asteria escaping the unwanted embrace of Zeus. Asteria shapeshifts in her attempts to avoid Zeus, with Zeus likewise taking on different forms as he chases her. Eventually, Asteria, as a quail, hurls herself into the ocean and takes on the form of a floating island. At this point, Zeus gives up the chase, later chasing after Asteria's sister, Leto, whom he impregnates with the twins. The island, which is the body of Asteria, would become the birthplace of the twins.

## Artemis & Guinea Fowl

Another ground bird, the guinea fowl (meleagris), featured in one of the stories of Artemis and her wrath. Artemis transformed the Meleagrides, princesses of Aitolia into guinea hens. The princesses were mourning the death of their brother at the hands of Artemis as a result of their father King Oineus' behaviour towards the goddess and she felt sorry for them and so transformed them.[239]

## Buzzard

As the goddess of the hunt, at least one bird of prey is expected to be sacred to her. Aelian describes the buzzard (triorkhes) as being sacred to Artemis.[240] There are different buzzard species, which are associated with Apollo and the messenger god Hermes.

## Goldfinch

Aristophanes associated the goldfinch with Artemis in his play The Birds, where the priest said:

> *"Pray to the swan of Delos [Apollo],*
> *to Latona the mother of quails [Leto], and to Artemis,*
> *the goldfinch."*

---

[239] Hyginus, Fabulae 172.
[240] Aelian, On Animals 12.4.

## Swan

Both Apollo and Artemis are associated with the swan. Swans lived in the river Erindanos in Hyperborea (a mythical place in the far north of eternal spring), where Apollo flew on the back of a swan for the winter months. The swans sang paeans to Apollo and circled his temple here, and the locals held a belief that their elderly were transformed into swans by bathing in the river swamps.

Figure 16 - Artemis with two swans, Corinthian perfume vase circa 620 BCE. Gift of L. P. di Cesnola, 1876 in the Metropolitan Museum of Art.

A vase image dating to the 5th century BCE shows Artemis feeding a swan, with her bow and quiver visible on her back.[241] A Corinthian perfume vase dated to around 590-620 BCE and attributed to the Potnia painter depicts Artemis holding two swans.

Swans were likewise associated with the goddess Aphrodite and may have symbolised beauty and grace.

---

241 Vase B2365, State Hermitage Museum, St Petersburg.

## ARTEMIS & BOARS

Like deer, the boar (hus) was sacred to Artemis. As the goddess of the hunt, Artemis could turn the hunted into the hunter. She did exactly this when she punished King Oineus of Calydon.

The King forgot to offer the first fruits to Artemis when he was making sacrifices to the Gods, and she punished him by making a savage giant boar ravage his lands. The King further angered Artemis by sending out a call for heroes to come and slay the savage Calydonian boar. After the boar was dead the King gave the meat of the boar to the heroes to eat, keeping the head and hide as his privilege. Because of its strength and ferocity, a boar would have been considered a worthy opponent for any hunter and therefore a giant boar was a great prize.

Artemis, obviously displeased at the killing of the boar, sowed discord amongst the hunters. She caused the sons of Thestio to seize the hide, and in declaring that it was their share of the spoils, a war broke out between their people (the Kouretes) and the heroes of the Calydonians who had also helped in the hunt.[242]

During the hunt for the boar, a prince of Arcadia, Ankaios, boasted that not even Artemis would stop him from slaying it. Artemis soon proved Ankaois wrong by making the boar slay him with its tusks. Another prince who offended Artemis with his boasts was Adonis, the lover of Aphrodite from the Mediterranean island of Cyprus, who she had killed in the same manner on the tusks of a wild boar.

The tale of the founding of Ephesus recounted by Herodotus attributes the location of Ephesus to the place where a boar was killed, fulfilling the words of the oracle that *"a fish and a boar will show you the way"*.

A remarkable tale recounts the dream of Phintias, ruler of Acragas, who dreamed that while hunting boar, he was slain by a wild sow. To appease Artemis, he had coins minted with her head

---

[242] Antoninus Liberalis, Metamorphoses; Ovid, Metamorphoses 2.

on one side and that of a wild boar on the reverse.243 This must have worked, as Phintias went on to live for some years afterwards.

## ARTEMIS & BULLS

Artemis was, on occasion, associated with bulls. Her title of *Tauropolos* indicates this, from the founding of the Taurean tribe in Skythia by Iphigeneia after a bull was substituted in her place by Artemis. It is also interesting to note that Theseus founded a temple to *Artemis Soteira* (Saviour) after slaying the Minotaur.244

Pausanias mentions a relief in front of the temple of Apollo at Argolis of a fight between a bull and a wolf, with a maiden thought to be Artemis throwing a rock at the bull.245

Several ancient Greek coins show Artemis riding bulls or with Artemis on the front and a bull on the reverse. Even bronze coins showed Artemis riding on the back of a leaping bull with a lunar crescent beneath.246

## ARTEMIS & DEER

*"Stag-hunter Artemis, on the hills thou dost eagerly hunt with fawn-killing Dionysus."*247

Artemis was often depicted with deer or stags in statues and images on reliefs. She was Elaphobolos, hunter of deer, though they could find sanctuary at her temples and shrines, and she would punish hunters who tried to kill pregnant deer.

Hera referred to Artemis' love of hunting deer when she hit her, telling her she would be better off hunting deer than fighting her superiors.248 This was perhaps unkind, as Artemis transformed herself into a deer to escape the Aloadai giants and caused them to kill each other, saving herself and Hera from their unwanted

---

243 Diodorus Siculus 22.5.
244 Pausanias 2.31.4.
245 Pausanias 2.19.7.
246 Zeus: A Study in Ancient Religion – Arthur Cook, volume 1:538, 1914.
247 Dionysiaca 44:198.
248 Iliad 21.470, see also Dionysiaca 44.198.

attentions.[249] Artemis also replaced Iphigeneia with a deer when she saved her from being sacrificed.

Four golden hinds pulled Artemis' chariot. The fifth was captured by Herakles (Hercules) as one of his labours, the capture of the Cerityneah Hind. [250] He wounded the hind and had to talk smoothly to Artemis to save himself from her wrath.[251] The goddess allowed him to take the hind to complete his labours.

As *Elaphiaia* (of the deer), it is not surprising that the symbol of the deer-drawn chariot was used in her rites to honour her. At her festival at Patrai, the priestess rode on a chariot drawn by deer in honour of Artemis.[252]

The Elaphebolos festival honouring Artemis Elaphiaia included making elaphos and cakes in the shape of deer or stags as offerings to Artemis.

Gold coins from the early 4th century BCE depicted Artemis riding on the back of a stag were found.[253] Along with the bull, the stag was the other main animal Artemis was shown riding on coins.

# ARTEMIS & DOGS

As a goddess of the hunt, Artemis did not always hunt alone. At times, she was accompanied by attendants, her pack of hunting hounds or by the beautiful god of wine and wildness, Dionysus, one of her closest friends among the gods.

The shepherd god Pan gave Artemis a gift of the finest hunting dogs. He gave her six dogs - two black and white dogs, three red ones and one spotted. He also gave her seven Kynosourian bitches, famed for their tracking and hunting skills.[254] It is interesting to note that the total of thirteen hounds is a lunar number. Dogs also have a long history of association with the moon.

---

249 Apollodorus 1.53.
250 Callimachus, Hymn 3 to Artemis.
251 Apollodorus 2.81.
252 Pausanias 7.18.8
253 Greek Coins – Charles Seltman, p181, 1933.
254 Callimachus, Hymn 3 to Artemis.

FIGURE 17 – ARTEMIS-BENDIS WITH A HERM OF PAN, 4TH CENTURY BCC, ATTIC. CORCORAN COLLECTION (WILLIAM A. CLARK COLLECTION). NATIONAL GALLERY OF ART.

Dogs are one of Artemis' best-known sacred animals. Many depictions of Artemis show her with a dog at her side and sometimes with her beloved hunting pack surrounding her. In ancient Greece, dogs were bred for hunting and were an expensive investment. It was believed that Artemis was responsible for the well-being of all these hunting dogs. Hekate is likewise shown and described as accompanied by dogs.

## ARTEMIS & FISH

Artemis also hunted fish, as implied by the use of the title Diktynna (of the nets), and seen in the Homeric Hymns.

There were references to many of Artemis' shrines having sacred springs, and she was also associated with lakes, through temples to Artemis Limnaia (Lady of the Lake), which were erected on the shores of lakes. As a result of this fresh-water fish were considered to be sacred to her, presumably as a different type of prey.[255]

The nymphs of Syracuse[256] were said to have caused a great fountain to gush forth to please Artemis, which contained fish in huge numbers that were held sacred to Artemis, and it was forbidden to remove them.[257] There was also a sacred spring at Syracuse, which was the nymph Arethousa after she had been transformed to save her from rape. This spring was said to contain a tame sacred eel.[258] It is likely that both these stories reference the Fountain of Arethousa on the islet of Ortygia, Syracuse where tourists still ponder the myths of the Goddess.

FIGURE 18 - MODERN SCULPTURE SHOWING THE NYMPH ARETHOUSA BEING PERSUED BY THE RIVER GOD. IT STANDS NEAR THE FOUNTAIN IN SICILY TODAY.

A fish figured in the founding of the city of Ephesus, where the largest and most famous temple of Artemis was located. The oracle had said "*a fish and a boar will show you the way*", and it was while the men were making a fire to cook the fish they had caught that a boar

---

255 Diodorus Siculus 5.2.3.
256 Modern day Sicily
*257 Diodorus Siculus 5.2.3-5.5.1.*
258 Aelian, On Animals 8.4.

was scared from the bushes and subsequently killed, providing the location at its death spot for the city.

## ARTEMIS & HARES

The hare is associated with Artemis through the foundation myth of the colony of Boiai. When they consulted an oracle, the settlers were told that the goddess would show them where to dwell, and then a hare appeared, guided the settlers to the spot, and disappeared into a myrtle tree.[259]

In Aeschylus' Agamemnon, the goddess was said to demand the sacrifice of Iphigeneia because she was angry that a pregnant hare was killed by an eagle near the palace of Agamemnon. This was also said to be an omen for the destruction of Troy, with the hare representing Troy and the eagle the avenging Greeks.

## ARTEMIS, LIONS & LEOPARDS

Both the lion and leopard were frequently depicted in association with Artemis. We find depictions of lions at Ephesus, one of her primary temples.[260] Pausanias describes Artemis holding a lion in her left hand and a leopard in her right[261], which may refer to images of Artemis such as that on an 8th century BCE vase found in Italy. Artemis is also shown wearing a leopard-skin cloak.[262]

This is also suggestive of the gods most important to Artemis – the lion as a symbol of Apollo and the leopard as a symbol of Dionysus.

Artemis was called a *"lion among women"* in the Iliad, further emphasizing the leonine connection.[263] Theocritus also uses leonine symbolism, describing the beasts going to the grove of Artemis,

---

[259] Pausanias 3.22.12.
[260] The Earlier Temple of Artemis at Ephesus – W.R. Lethaby, Journal of Hellenic Studies, 1917 1:1-16.
[261] Pausanias 5.19.5.
[262] Vase B2365, State Hermitage Museum, St Petersburg.
[263] Iliad 21.470.

where there is a lioness at the centre, and then compares Artemis to the lioness.[264]

> *"The Child of Zeus, the tireless Huntress Artemis sleeping, what time her feet forwearied are with following lions with her flying shafts over the hills far-stretching."*[265]

Artemis is depicted hunting a large feline on a 7th century BCE Corinthian vase. It is unclear whether this is a lion or a leopard, but it demonstrates that the big cat motif was evident early on. As a solar beast, we might expect to see the lion more connected with Apollo, but this was not the case until centuries later, reinforcing the strength of the Artemis-lion connection.

Although the leopard was traditionally sacred to Dionysus, we may also note that it was seen frequently in company with Artemis. The temple of Artemis at Corfu had a central winged figure flanked by two leopards over the entrance. This figure is often described as a Gorgo (hideous apotropaic figure akin to a Sheela-na-gig) and may have been a masked figure of Artemis herself. The use of grotesque initiation masks in ceremonies has been suggested from masks found at the sanctuary of Artemis Orthia in Sparta.[266]

An 8th century BCE vase from Italy showed Artemis as Queen of the Beasts with a leopard in one hand and a stag in the other.[267] This is a common theme in early vases, *"in the seventh century (BCE) she had been shown as a Mistress of Animals, often winged, holding one or two beasts, usually lions."*[268] A 5th century BCE vase shows Artemis wearing a leopard-skin cloak, feeding a swan.[269] A leopard cub is depicted on a 5th century BCE vase that shows Artemis with her brother Apollo and mother Leto.[270] The association of the leopard with Artemis (the ultimate huntress) may be due to its effectiveness as a hunter.

---

264 Theocritus, Theocritus.
265 Quintus Smyrnaeus, Fall of Troy 1.905.
266 See The Sanctuary of Artemis Orthia at Sparta – R.D. Dawkins, in Journal of Hellenic Studies 5, 1929.
267 Vase 4209, Museo Archeologico Nazionale, Florence.
268 Athenian Black Figure Vases – John Boardman, p219, 1974.
269 Vase B2365, State Hermitage Museum, St Petersburg.
270 Vase E256, British Museum, London.

The lion theme is continued in the Drachms (gold coins) issued in Massilia in the 4th century BCE, which had the head of Artemis on one side and a lion on the reverse.[271] These coins, which were frequently copied, became the chief currency of Southern Gaul at this time.

## ARTEMIS & SERPENTS

The twin serpent motif is also seen in association with Artemis, on coins, at temples in friezes, and in statues.

A coin from Aureliopos in Lydia shows Artemis with a crescent moon on her head in a chariot drawn by two snakes (2nd century BCE).[272] The Gorgo figure at Corfu also has twin serpents at her waist, rearing to face each other, repeating the motif of twin serpents. Pausanias describes a statue of the goddess in the temple of Artemis at Despoine in Arcadia. The statue is described as being a bronze image of her bearing a torch in one hand and two serpents in the other.[273] Another serpent reference is found in Apollodorus, recounting how Artemis punished Admetos for neglecting her.

> *"While making his matrimonial sacrifices, Admetos forgot to include one for Artemis. Consequently, when he opened the door to the bridal chamber, he found it full of the coils of serpents. Apollo told him how to propitiate the goddess."*[274]

## ARTEMIS & WOLVES

The wolf is the sacred animal of Apollo, but as an effective hunter, it was also sacred to Artemis, as Artemis *Lykeii*, which translates as *of the wolves*. This is reinforced in a late text by the Roman writer Oppian, who categorised wolves into five types:

- the Archer (large and tawny)
- the Falcon (large and silvery)

---

271 Greek Coins – Charles Seltman, p196, 1933.
272 Zeus 1:245.
273 Pausanias 8.37.1.
274 Apollodorus 1.105.

- the Golden Wolf (very large)
- the Kite (small and silvery)
- an unnamed class (small and dark).[275]

That a type of wolf should be called Archer strongly hints at a connection to Artemis, as does the Golden wolf, considering the number of titles she had with the word "golden" in.

Additionally, wolves were sacred to her mother, Leto, who provided her with safety when she was pregnant with Artemis and Apollo. In a later account by Liberalis (circa 100-300 CE), Leto came from Hyperborea as a she-wolf. In an alternative version, she came from Lycia, named for the wolves that cared for her.

---

[275] Oppian, Cynegetica 3:300-301 (212 CE).

# 10.
# GODDESS OF THE DANCE & SONG

*But the goddess with a bold heart turns every way destroying the race of wild beasts: and when she is satisfied and has cheered her heart, this huntress who delights in arrows slackens her supple bow and goes to the great house of her dear brother Phoebus Apollo, to the rich land of Delphi, there to order the lovely dance of the Muses and Graces. There she hangs up her curved bow and her arrows, and heads and leads the dances, gracefully arrayed, while all they utter their heavenly voice, singing how neat-ankled Leto bare children supreme among the immortals both in thought and in deed.*

Hymn 27, Homeric Hymn to Artemis. Translation by H. Evelyn-White

Artemis had a strong association with dance and song. In the Homeric Hymns, Artemis leads the dances of the Muses and Graces in Apollo's Delphi while they all sing.[276] Artemis is not only the leader of the dance but also of the choregos or leader of the choir. The Homeric Hymn to Aphrodite also referred to Artemis loving dancing, as well as the lyre and strong-voiced song.[277] The Homeric Hymn to Pythian Apollo[278] mentions Artemis Iokheaira singing with the Muses. Pausanias mentions the annual dancing and choral singing at Karyai in Lacedaemon around an image of Artemis set out in the open.[279] The dance performed by the maidens was known as the Karyatis and was described as a spirited jig with many pirouettes and whirls.

---

[276] Homeric Hymn 27 to Artemis.
[277] Homeric Hymn 5 to Aphrodite.
[278] Homeric Hymn 3 to Apollo.
[279] Pausanias 3.10.7.

# ALKMAN'S HYMN TO ARTEMIS OF THE STRICT OBSERVANCE

One of the oldest choral songs known is from the 7th century BCE Sparta, by the poet Alkman. It is entitled *A Hymn to Artemis of the Strict Observance* and is described as being for a chorus of Spartan girls dressed as doves to sing at dawn on the Feast of the Plough.

*'I am your servant, Artemis.*
*You draw your long bow at night,*
*clothed in the skins of wild beasts.*
*Now hear our beautiful singing.'*[280]

The reference to doves may well indicate the girls should be dressed as nymphs, as the word doves is a translation of the Pleiades, the seven nymph sisters who were companions of Artemis for a while. The Pleiades were the sacred women of the god Zeus and the goddess Dione. They were associated with the oracle at Dodona, an ancient and highly regarded oracle. Dione is a mysterious goddess whose name means *Goddess*; she is variously linked to the goddesses Diana (which also means *Goddess* or *Holy Woman*), Hekate, Aphrodite (as her mother), Asherah and a Phoenician goddess connected to the city of Byblos.

# PAEAN

A form of choral song that must be considered is the paean, which is distinct from choral hymns. Originally, paeans were songs of gratitude or propitiation sung to Artemis or Apollo - and on occasion to Hekate; later, they were also offered to some other deities such as Dionysus, Helios and Asclepius (all of whom have a close association with Apollo).

In the earliest example, they were sung by young men with young women supplying the ritual cries, but they were subsequently performed by young women choruses. Euripides describes Iphigeneia asking a chorus of girls from Chalcis to sing a propitiating paean to Artemis while moving around her temple and altar.[281]

---

280 Alkman of Sparta, c. 625 BCE.
281 Euripides, Iphigeneia at Aulis, 1467, 1480.

Sophocles also refers to young girls singing a paean to Artemis and her nymphs.[282]

The name *Paean* was also given to a physician god equated with Apollo, who was said to be the physician to the gods. Apollo continued to be closely associated with healing through his son Asclepius, the God of Healing.

## THE KORDAX

While singing is mentioned occasionally, dance seems to have been more significant. Dances likely played an essential part in some of the ceremonies of Artemis. It was said of her, *"Where has not Artemis danced?"*[283] We see her given titles such as Kordax (a dance from Lydia), and in the Greek Magical Papyri, she is called with the phrase *"O song and dance"*.[284]

The Kordax is the subject of much debate. It is known that this dance was sacred to Artemis[285], but it has been suggested that it was either a circle dance or a sinuous serpentine-type dance without moving the feet. A gloss by Hesychius refers to Spartan women dancers called *korythalistriai*, who danced at a festival for Artemis Korythalia.

## CIRCLE DANCING

Callimachus refers to Artemis several times in association with dance, saying: *"[Artemis] whose study is the bow ... and the spacious dance"*, and *"when the Nymphs encircle thee in the dance"*, going on to remark that the sun god Helios paused to watch her dance in the mid-summer, causing the day to lengthen.[286]

It is not surprising that her maidens danced at Ephesus or that young girls had to dance as the she-bear at Brauron. At the Temple of Ephesus, the maidens were said to *"sport and lightly leap and clap*

---

282 Sophocles, Trojan Women.
283 Proverbia Aesopi No 9, p229.
284 PGM VII:686-702.
285 Pausanias 6.22.1.
286 Callimachus, Hymn 3 to Artemis.

*their hands in the temple of Artemis the Fair at Ephesos, now sinking down upon their haunches and again springing up, like the hopping wagtail."*[287]

Choral singing was frequently performed with the participants standing in a circle, hence the reference in Callimachus to the nymphs encircling Artemis in the dance.[288] Similarly, the chorus in Euripides' Trojan Women refers to dancing around the temple of Artemis to honour her.[289]

This passage from the Iliad illustrates how dancing and singing in honour of Artemis may have been performed together:

*"He watched her with his eyes among the girls dancing in the choir for Artemis Khryselakatos Keladeine."*[290]

The choregos would stand in the centre of the circle and be distinguished by her beauty. We see the comparison of Princess Nausicaa to Artemis when she stands amongst her attendants as choregos.[291] Also referenced in the Ephesiaca is the beautiful maiden Antheia, who directs the other maidens and is mistaken for Artemis by the crowds because of her outstanding beauty and height.[292] Artemis as the choregos was consistent with the Delian ritual performance of hymns, as referred to in works like Euripides' Hecuba.[293]

# WAR DANCING & THE AMAZONS

Weapon dances are represented in Greek art from as early as the 8th century BCE and were mainly disseminated from Crete and Sparta. The dancers of such dances were known as pyrrichists. The most widely represented group of pyrrichists is female.[294] Pyrrichists performed nude with helmets, greaves, a shield and a weapon such as a sword, spear or javelin.

---

287 Aelian, On Animals 12.9.
288 Callimachus, Hymn 3 to Artemis.
289 Euripides, Trojan Women, 551.
*290 Iliad 16.181.*
291 Odyssey 6.151.
292 Xenophon, Ephesiaca.
293 Dance and Ritual Play in Greek Religion – Stephen Lonsdale, p66.
294 Dance and Ritual Play in Greek Religion – Stephen Lonsdale, p144.

The origins of the war dances are hinted at by Callimachus, who wrote:

> *"the Amazons ... and Hippo [their Queen] performed a holy rite for thee, and they .... around the image danced a war-dance - first in shields and armour, and again in a circle arraying a spacious choir."*[295]

This concurs with tales of the Amazons as the founders of the town of Pyrrhikhos in Lacedaemon, as the term *pyrrichist* may well be derived from *Pyrrhikhos*. Hippolyta (Hippo), Queen of the Amazons, was turned into a horse by Artemis for refusing to perform the annual dance around the altar at Ephesus.[296]

An Attic vase from around 440 BCE shows Artemis carrying her bow and a long torch with a dancing male pyrrichist in front of her.[297]

# ABDUCTION FROM THE DANCE

In the Homeric Hymn 5 to Aphrodite, the goddess denies being immortal as part of her efforts to lure a young man into her bed. Aphrodite describes herself as having been abducted from the dance of the huntress Artemis, of the golden arrows.[298]

This theme of abduction of the dancing maidens from an Artemis temple or ceremony was common. Herodotus refers to the abduction by raiding Pelasgians of Athenian women from Brauron while they were celebrating the festival of Artemis there.[299] Plutarch describes the abduction of Helen by Theseus and Peirithous when she was dancing in the sanctuary of Artemis Orthia. Pausanias also reports the abduction of girls performing dances for Artemis Karyae at Sparta by the hero Aristomenes and his men.[300]

---

295 Callimachus, Hymn 3 to Artemis.
296 Callimachus Hymn 3 to Artemis.
297 Museo Archeologico Nazionale, Naples, 81908 (H3010), cat no 6.40.
298 Homeric Hymn 5 to Aphrodite.
299 Herodotus 6.138.
300 Pausanias 4.16.9.

When some of his men get drunk and try to rape the virgins, Aristomenes kills them and ransoms the girls back unharmed, possibly to avoid the wrath of Artemis.

We may also note that Persephone was in the company of the virgin goddesses Artemis and Athena and many nymphs when Hades abducted her.[301]

---

[301] Homeric Hymn 2 to Demeter, Pausanias 8.31.2.

# 11.
# GODDESS OF WATER

*Come with bows bent and with emptying of quivers,*
*Maiden most perfect, lady of light,*
*With a noise of winds and many rivers,*
*With a clamour of waters, and with might;*
*Bind on thy sandals, O thou most fleet,*
*Over the splendour and speed of thy feet;*
*For the faint east quickens, the wan west shivers,*
*Round the feet of the day and the feet of the night.*
Atalanta in Calydon, Algernon Charles Swinburne, 1865

Artemis is strongly associated with water, as the Lady of the Lake, Artemis *Limnaia*. There were several shrines to Artemis with this title, and sacred springs and pools were prominent at Artemis' temples. She demonstrated her power over water several times by turning people into springs.

Artemis saw Pan chasing her nymph companion Pholoe and transformed Pholoe into a spring to escape the god's unwanted attention.[302]

The nymph Arethousa prayed to Artemis for help when fleeing the unwanted attentions of the river god Alpheios. Arethousa had been a loyal devotee of Artemis, so the goddess transformed Arethousa into a spring and took her to the precinct of her shrine on Ortygia, Syracuse (Sicily). This spring contained a tame sacred eel that accepted food.[303] Subsequently, the priests of Artemis *Soteira* at Aegium performed a ritual of throwing offering cakes into the sea, saying that they were sending them to Arethousa in Syracuse. The implication is that Artemis would ensure the cakes travelled across the waters of the sea to the spring at Syracuse.[304]

---

302 Silvae 2.3.1.
303 Aelian, On Animals 8.4.
304 Pausanias 7.24.3.

Peirene, another nymph from Corinthos in Southern Greece, was also turned into a spring by Artemis. Artemis had accidentally killed Peirene's son, and the nymph was inconsolable. Artemis, feeling sorry for Peirene, transformed her into a fountain-spring so she could weep eternally.[305]

Zeus also made Artemis the goddess of roads and harbours, tying her in as a goddess of the ways, a role shared with Hekate. Callimachus described her as the *"Watcher over roads and harbours."*[306]

In the Argonautica, Artemis is described as the *"saviour of ships"* when a song is sung in her honour.[307]

FIGURE 19 – ATTIC RED-FIGURE LEKYTHOS, CA. 475 BCE, FROM SELINUNTE, SICILY. ANTONINO SALINAS REGIONAL ARCHAEOLOGICAL MUSEUM, PALERMO. PHOTO D'ESTE, 2023

---

305 Pausanias 2.3.2.
306 Callimachus, Hymn 3 to Artemis.
307 Argonautica 2.570.

# 12.
# WARRIOR GODDESS

Several historical accounts exist where Artemis received gratitude for her involvement in warfare, contributing to or guaranteeing victory. This is why the Greeks paid homage to her for her role in the Battle of Artemision, and the Athenians offered annual goat sacrifices in recognition of her assistance securing victory at Marathon.

Xenophon described long lines of soldiers marching from the gymnasiums to dedicate their wreaths to Artemis in Ephesus.[308] Strabo describes carvings on the pillar of the temple at Amarynthos, showing the Artemis festival procession, which contained three thousand soldiers, six hundred horsemen, and sixty chariots, emphasising her martial connection.[309]

Artemis herself was not averse to fighting in battle, as was shown by her participation in the Indian Wars of Dionysus and in the defence of Olympus against the giants when she slew the giant Aigaion with her arrows.[310]

Artemis was one of the patrons of the Amazons, along with the war god Ares. The Amazons were reputed to have founded several famous shrines to Artemis, including the temple at Ephesus[311] and the temple at Pyrrhikhos in Lacedaemon.[312] Artemis was particularly honoured at Sparta, the most martial of Greek cities. There were temples to her as Artemis *Diktynna*, Artemis *Aiginaii*, Artemis *Issoria*, Artemis *Hígemoni*, Artemis *Knagia*, Artemis *Korythalia* and the most significant, Artemis *Orthia*. The temple of Artemis at Euboia had an inscription on one of the pillars honouring the nearby battle that had occurred:

---

308 Xenophon, Agesilaus.
309 Strabo 10.1.10.
310 Apollodorus 1.38.
311 Pausanias 7.2.6.
312 Pausanias 3.25.3.

> "With numerous tribes from Asia's regions brought
> The sons of Athens on these waters, fought;
> Erecting, after they had quelled the Mede,
> To Artemis this record of the deed." [313]

Weapon dances were also associated with Artemis, as shown in an Attic vase from around 440 BCE, which shows Artemis carrying her bow and a long torch with a dancing male pyrrichist in front of her.[314] The war dances may well have begun with the Amazons, as Callimachus hinted at.[315] The Amazons worshipped Artemis as one of their tutelary deities, along with Ares.

---

313 Plutarch, Lives.
314 Museo Archeologico Nazionale, Naples, 81908 (H3010), cat no 6.40.
315 Callimachus, Hymn 3 to Artemis.

# 13.
# THE REVENGE OF ARTEMIS

Artemis frequently displayed a wrathful side to her nature. In many instances, there was a justified reason for this, and parallels can be drawn between Artemis and the goddess Nemesis, as both are seen dispensing divine vengeance.

In his Hymn 3 to Artemis, Callimachus summarises the actions that incur her wrath. These include:

- dishonouring her altar
- disputing her supremacy as an archer or huntress
- attempting to seduce her
- not attending her annual dance [316]

Artemis was also very protective of her mother, Leto, and would, with her twin brother Apollo, take revenge on all those who turned her mother away when she was pregnant. Again, it is with her brother that she revenges her mother's pride against the harsh words spoken by Queen Niobe, killing her children and against the giant Tityos, who tries to force himself on Leto. These incidents illustrate the importance that Artemis placed on her family relationships.

Artemis could also be appealed to as a fierce and wrathful goddess for protection.

> *"Artemis ... give ear to my prayers and ward off the evil Keres [Death-Spirits]. For you, goddess, this is no small thing, but for me it is critical."*[317]
>
> *"Philerátis dedicated this image to Artemis. Accept it, Lady, and watch over her safety."*[318]

---

316 Callimachus, Hymn 3 to Artemis.
317 Theognis 1.11.
318 Callimachus, Epigram 31.

# ACTAEON

Actaeon (or Aktaion) was a prince of Thebes and a keen hunter who had the misfortune of deciding to watch Artemis as she bathed naked in a stream. In her fury, Artemis transformed him into a stag, and he was slain by his own hounds.[319] A nymph spotted Actaeon hiding in his tree and screamed, alerting Artemis, who slid under the water to cover herself. Artemis made his dogs kill him slowly while he retained his human awareness as punishment for seeking to see her naked.[320]

# ADONIS

Adonis, the Cyprian prince and lover of Aphrodite, offended Artemis by saying that he was a better hunter than the goddess. She responded by sending a boar to gore and kill him.[321] This was a contributory factor to the ongoing feud between Aphrodite and Artemis.

# ARISTOMELIDAS

Artemis provoked the hero Khronios to slay King Aristomelidas after he defiled a maiden, making Khronios the strong arm of her vengeance. After killing the King, Khronios fled to Tegea and set up a sanctuary for Artemis, displaying unusually good sense for a hero.[322]

# BOUPHAGOS

Artemis was famous for her chastity, which some foolish mortals took as an enticing challenge. Unfortunately for them, the inevitable consequence of trying to molest Artemis was death, as shown in the tale of Bouphagos, who attempted to rape her and was killed for his attempt at irreverence.[323]

---

319 Hyginus Fabulae 181; Ovid, Metamorphoses 3.138; Apollodorus, The Library 3.30, Callimachus Hymn 5.106, The Bath of Pallas.
320 Dionysiaca 5.305-336.
321 Apollodorus 3.183.
322 Pausanias 8.47.6.
323 Pausanias 8.27.17.

# HIPPOLYTA

The Amazonian Queen Hippo (or Hippolyta) was said to have founded the shrine of Artemis at Ephesus with her fellow Amazons. However, when she refuses to dance around the altar, Artemis becomes furious and transforms Hippo into her namesake - a horse.[324]

# KORONIS

Koronis was a Princess of Trikka in Thessalia who was beloved of Apollo. She slept with another man during her pregnancy by Apollo, and Artemis killed her during the labour with her arrows for the insult to her brother. A different version of the myth has Artemis killing Koronis as a reprisal for Apollo's subterfuge in causing the death of Orion.

Artemis also killed many of Koronis' neighbours for not keeping a better eye on her.[325] While Koronis' body was burning on the funeral pyre, the god Hermes snatched her child from the flames.[326] This child was Asclepius, the God of Healing.

# LEIMON

Artemis and Apollo always held in their hearts the memory of their mother, Leto's challenging journey during her pregnancy. Almost everywhere she sought refuge, she faced rejection. Only the islands of Kos and Delos (Ortygia) extended a warm welcome to the pregnant goddess.

Some rulers did try and make amends, but even that did not go well. While Prince Skephros was apologizing to Apollo, his brother Prince Leimon came rushing in and killed him in fear that he was being accused. Artemis immediately killed Leimon in vengeance.[327]

---

324 Callimachus, Hymn 3 to Artemis.
325 Pindar, Pythian 3.
326 Pausanias 2.26.6.
327 Pausanias 8.53.1.

## LOMAITHO AND MELANIPPOS

The priestess Lomaitho not only broke her vows of chastity when she decided to make love to Melanippos, but she defiled the temple of the goddess by doing so in the inner sanctuary of Artemis' temple at Patrai.

Artemis made her wrath known to the two lovers and the entire population. The earth yielded no harvests, and strange and fatal diseases began to afflict the population. The people went to the Delphic Oracle, and the Pythian priestess revealed that the cause of their trouble started with the profane actions of the lovers. The Pythia ordered the sacrifice of the lovers to Artemis and demanded that the most beautiful young girl and boy be sacrificed to Artemis each year. From these human sacrifices, the river flowing by the sanctuary became the Ameilikhos (Relentless).[328]

## THE DAUGHTERS OF NIOBE

At the request of her mother, Leto, Artemis killed six of the seven daughters of Queen Niobe as punishment to the queen for boasting that she was more blessed than Leto due to her large number of children (seven sons and seven daughters).

Also see Queen Niobe of Thebes in chapter 5.

## PYTHON

The Python was a giant serpent or dragon that guarded the shrine of Delphi. During her pregnancy, Python pursued Leto across the lands at Hera's request. After their birth, Apollo and Artemis killed the Python with arrows (some versions attribute this slaying to Apollo only). Apollo then became the God of the Delphic Oracle.

After killing the Python, Artemis and Apollo punished the Corinthians for turning them away when they had come seeking purification for the killing of the ancient beast. Delphi then became a place of ritual purification under Apollo, removing the need to rely on any other place for purification.

---

328 Pausanias 7.19.1.

Artemis would not hesitate to strike down the wrong-doer with her arrows, disease, or sudden death if she was angered.

> *"Artemis Khrysenios killed Ladomeia
> the daughter of Bellerophontes in anger."* [329]

Artemis was always ready to slay humans who had offended the gods she cared most about, especially her mother, Leto, her brother Apollo and her hunting partner Dionysus.

> *"Tityos saw Leto when she came to Pytho and in a fit
> of passion tried to embrace her. But she called out to
> her children [Artemis & Apollo], who shot him dead
> with arrows. He is being punished even in death, for
> vultures feast on his heart in Hades' realm."* [330]

As a god of the wilds worshipped primarily by women, it makes sense that Dionysus would be friends with Artemis. Neither spent much time away from the wilds and enjoyed hunting and dancing. In a version of the tale of Ariadne, Artemis kills her for betraying Dionysus.[331]

Artemis frequently sent disease to punish those who had offended her. In this, Artemis is similar to the Egyptian lioness goddess Sekhmet, who could either heal or send disease through her seven arrows.

> *"And both infectious diseases and sudden deaths are
> attributed to these gods"* [332]

---

329 Iliad 6.205.
330 Apollodorus 1.22.
331 Odyssey 11.324.
332 Strabo 14.1.6.

# 14.
# THE BRIGHT SHINING MOON

Artemis is associated with all the phases of the moon, but especially the new and full moon. The light of the Moon can sometimes appear to have a golden glow and, at others, a silvery white glow, and this is likely why Artemis' attire and weapons are described as golden or silver in appearance. In the later period, icons of the goddess depicted her with a lunar crescent on her head, reinforcing her associations with the moon. This was especially prominent during the Roman era when Artemis became synonymous with Diana, the Roman Goddess of the hunt and moon.

The Greek Lyric fragments associate Artemis with the moon, recounting that Artemis would provide particularly easy childbirth at the full moon to people and animals.[333] These full moon references hint at the conflation between Artemis and Selene, as the latter was particularly associated with the full moon.

In the Dionysiaca, the shade of the dying Actaeon describes Artemis to his father as *"the full moon of evening flashing through the water"*.[334]

In the 2nd century BCE the Stoics, in *Apollodorus Stoic 40* and *Diogenes Bab Diels Doxogr 549 b7* also associates Artemis with the Moon. By the time of Plutarch (Quaest Conv 659) in the 1st to 2nd-century CE, it is taken as read that Artemis is a lunar goddess.

## SELENE AND ARTEMIS

Artemis also assumes many of the powers and associations of the Hellenic goddess of the moon, Selene, which provides further reasons for considering her a lunar goddess. Selene was the lunar counterpart to Helios. In this pairing, Selene was the Moon and Helios the Sun, riding through the sky and illuminating the sky in an

---

333 Greek Lyric I Alcaeus Frag 390 (from Scholiast on Iliad).
334 Dionysiaca 5.485

eternal chase. In later eras, Artemis' cults incorporated Selene's worship and qualities, while Apollo's took on many of the qualities and roles of Helios.

## OF GOLD & SILVER

Artemis' golden bow and arrows could be used not only for killing the animals she hunted but also to bring disease and sudden death to people.

Artemis' chariot was golden and was pulled by four giant golden-horned deer. These deer were captured by Artemis when she was very young and were the first prey she ever hunted. All of the tracery (reins, yokes, etc) of her chariot were also golden.[335]

The title *Khryselakatos* refers to arrows *with shafts of gold*. This title is an early reference in the Iliad and Homeric Hymns. The Homeric Hymn 27 to Artemis refers to her golden bow, saying of her, *"Over the shadowy hills and windy peaks she draws her golden bow."* Ovid also refers to the golden bow, writing in his Metamorphoses, *"Syrinx revered Ortygia [Artemis]; girt like her she well might seem, so easy to mistake ... were not her bow of horn, Latonia's gold."*[336]

In Hymn 3 of Callimachus, we find, *"And how often goddess, didst thou make trial of thy silver bow?"*[337] The Contest of Homer and Hesiod refers to her bow as silver, *"[Artemis] slew Callisto with a shot of her silver bow."*[338]

The bow in these descriptions describes both Artemis' physical bow and the visible symbol of the golden light of the lunar crescent as it rides through the night sky. While we associate silver with the Moon today, the glow of the Moon is also often perceived by the naked eye as having a golden glow.

---

335 Callimachus, Hymn 3 to Artemis.
336 Ovid, Metamorphoses, 1.693.
337 Callimachus, Hymn 3 to Artemis.
338 Of the Origins of Homer and Hesiod, And of Their Contest 316.

Herodotus uses the epithet Khrysaoros (golden-sworded)[339] for Artemis when describing the words of an oracle predicting the outcome of the Persian Wars.[340]

In the Homeric Hymn, *"[Artemis] swiftly drives her all-golden chariot,"* pulled by four golden-horned deer. The chariot is likely an attribute that Artemis inherited from Selene, who also drives a chariot. Some writers describe Selene's chariot as silver, while others, including Pindar, describe it as golden. Though it is worth noting that Selene's chariot is pulled by two white horses, it is drawn by oxen or bulls, whereas Artemis' is drawn by deer.

The golden chariot is emphasised in 3rd century BCE Hymn 3 to Artemis by Callimachus:

> *"Artemis, Virgin, Slayer of Tityos, golden were your arms and golden your belt, you yoked a golden chariot, and golden bridles, you put on your deer."* [341]

The golden tracery of her chariot probably led to the title of *Khrysenios (of the golden reins)*, found in the Iliad.[342] This title is also used for the god Ares in Homer's Odyssey.

# THE LIGHT-BRINGER

Artemis asked Zeus to make her the light-bringer in Callimachus' Hymn to Artemis, saying, *"give me to be Phaesphoria [Bringer of Light]"*.[343] Many of her epithets also indicate a connection to light and brightness attributes that Artemis shares with the goddesses Hekate and Phoebe.

In the Dionysiaca, Artemis is described *"diffusing radiance from her face"* and saying she was also known as the *"fair-faced Bringer of Light."*[344]

---

339 See e.g. Homeric Hymn 27 to Artemis.
340 Herodotus 8.77.
341 Callimachus, Hymn 3 to Artemis.
342 Iliad 6.205.
343 Callimachus, Hymn 3 to Artemis.
344 Callimachus, Hymn 3 to Artemis 188.

Sophocles' Oedipus the King references *"winged with fire, the rays of Artemis, with which, on Lycian hills, she moveth on her course"*.[345]

Even more blatant than this is her title of Aithopia (burning-faced one), which seems to directly describe radiance. A reference in Callimachus also refers to the *"unquenchable light of fire"*.

The reference by Athenaios that amphiphontes cakes were offered at the temples of Artemis and at crossroads when the sky was lit by both the sun and the moon from either side suggests a joining of both sun and moon in the celebration of Artemis.[346] The sun and moon are usually visible in the sky for part of the month at sunrise and part at sunset, except for the period around New Moon.

Artemis is also referred to by the title of *Phoebe* (Light). In this, she pairs her brother Apollo, who is given the epithet *Phoebus*. This attribute may have been inherited from their grandmother, the titan goddess Phoebe, mother to Leto and Asteria. Phoebe was the daughter of Ouranos and Gaia and held the position of goddess of the Oracle temple at Delphi before it passed to her grandson Apollo.

Artemis, like Hekate who shares the title of *Phosphoros* with her, is associated with torches and fire. In Callimachus, we find this evocative description suggesting that the light of fire is also associated with her:

> *"And where did you cut the pine for torches, lit by
> what flame? It was on Mysian Olympus, you breathed
> into the torches the unquenchable light of fire..."* [347]

A sanctuary on Mount Krathis was dedicated to Artemis Pyronia, the *Fire Goddess*. Fire from this sanctuary was said to be used in Lernaian ceremonies to the Hydra.

Artemis' association with gold continues when she is given the title of *Khrysothronos*, which means *golden-throned* in both the Iliad[348] and the Odyssey.[349]

---

345 Sophocles, Oedipus the King 216-19.
346 Athenaios, Deipnosophistai 14.645a.
347 Callimachus, Hymn 3 to Artemis.
348 Iliad 9.530.
349 Odyssey 5.119.

# 15.
# DIVINE RELATIONSHIPS

Artemis' relationships with other deities include familial relationships, friendships, goddesses with whom she is conflated or confused, and also the deities with whom she had hostile relationships.

## ARTEMIS & APHRODITE

There was, not surprisingly, a lot of hostility between these two goddesses. Artemis was one of the three goddesses unaffected by Aphrodite's powers, the others being the virgin goddesses Athena and Hestia. Aphrodite was angered by this as the young people who dedicated themselves to Artemis were often the most beautiful ones, for example, Atalanta and Hippolytus.

To make matters worse, Prince Hippolytus, a favourite of Artemis, was slain through the wiles of Aphrodite.[350] The rivalry plays out in Euripides' Hippolytus, where Aphrodite has Hippolytus killed for spurning love and devoting himself to Artemis with a life of celibacy and hunting. In retaliation, Artemis sent a boar after Adonis, the lover of Aphrodite, wounding and killing him.[351]

Aphrodite was also responsible for the loss through rape, death or marriage of several of the companions of Artemis, including Syrinx, Polyphonte and Atalanta.

Some readers may find it interesting that Aphrodite was also sometimes depicted with the pillar-type body seen on Artemis of Ephesus in Asia Minor. The best-known examples are from the Roman city of Aphrodisias, showing Aphrodite with the pillar-type body on which various symbols associated with her are shown.

---

350 Pausanias 2.27.4.
351 Apollodorus 3.183.

FIGURE 20 - APHRODITE OF APHRODISIAS, AYDIN PROVINCE, TURKIYE –
NOW ON DISPLAY IN THE ARCHAEOLOGICAL MUSEUM IN ISTANBUL.

# ARTEMIS & APOLLO

As twins, Artemis and Apollo were understandably very close. Their bond begins at birth, with Artemis assisting in the birth of Apollo shortly after her own birth. The two were usually shown seated together in images of Olympus. Callimachus said that although all the gods invited her to sit next to them, Artemis always chose to sit with Apollo.[352]

Together, the twins were very protective of their mother, the goddess Leto. They killed the Python of Delphi, which had chased her when she was pregnant and punished the many people who refused her shelter as she was fleeing. They also slew the giant Tityos for trying to molest their mother and the children of Queen Niobe after she boasted she was more blessed than Leto and offended her.

The twins shared several roles and titles as well. They were both protectors of young children - Artemis for the girls and Apollo for the boys. They shared the title *Light*, Artemis as Phoebe and Apollo

---

352 Callimachus, Hymn 3 to Artemis.

as the male version of Phoebus. They both could send pestilence as well as sudden death. [353]

The festival of Thargelia (First Fruits) celebrated their birth on the 6th and 7th Thargelion, respectively. Apollo and Artemis were both patrons of the Hyperboreoi.

A good example of a curse involving Artemis from the 6th century BCE gives her acting in conjunction with her brother Apollo, their mother Leto and the goddess of wisdom Athena. This curse is actually part of an oath called the Amphictyonic oath, and refers to an obligation not to till the sacred plain of Cirrha.

> *"Let them be under the curse of Apollo and Artemis and Leto and Athena Pronaea. The curse goes on: that their land bear no fruit that their wives bear children not like those who begat them, but monsters; that their flocks yield not their natural increase; that defeat awaits them in camp and court and market place; and that they perish utterly, themselves, their houses, their whole race. And never may they offer pure sacrifice unto Apollo, nor to Artemis, nor to Leto, nor to Athena Pronaea, and may the gods refuse their offerings."* [354]

## ARTEMIS & ARES

Artemis and Ares were both significant deities of the Amazons. Artemis and Ares were honoured together at Ilissos in Athens. Artemis Agrotera and Ares Enyalios were also honoured at the festival of Charisteria, which celebrated the victory over the Persians at the battle of Marathon.

Hyginus recorded that the mythical Amazon queen Otrera, a wife of Ares, was the founder of the temple of Artemis at Ephesus.[355] It is also interesting to observe that Ares was said to have provided a flock of birds which shot arrows from their feathers to guard the island sanctuary of the Amazons.[356]

---

353 Strabo 14.1.6.
354 The Speeches of Aeschines, Aeshin, Or. 3.111; translation by Ch.D. Adams.
355 Hyginus, Fabulae 223, 225
356 Hyginus, Fabulae 30.

Another connection between these two deities is through the pyrrichists (war dancers), who danced in war gear with weapons, connecting the god of war to Artemis as the goddess of the dance.

## ARTEMIS, ATHENA & PERSEPHONE

The virgin goddesses Athena and Persephone were raised with Artemis on Sicily, until the taking of Persephone by Hades. The three maidens wove Zeus' robe and gathered flowers. Because of their happy memories of this time, this island was said to be the favourite of these goddesses.[357] The three maidens were all said to have been gathering flowers with nymphs when Hades rose from the underworld in his chariot and abducted Persephone.[358]

## ARTEMIS & AURA

Aura, the Titan goddess of the breeze and the cool air of the morning was Artemis' close companion. She even received the honour of riding in Artemis' chariot with her.[359] However, the sword and proud virgin attendant fell out of favour with Artemis when she insulted her. This is recounted by Nonnus in the Dionysiaca, where Aura speaks and compares Artemis to Aphrodite, insinuating she was too feminine to be a virgin goddess:

> *"Artemis, you only have the name of a virgin maid,*
> *because your rounded breasts are full and soft, a*
> *woman's breasts like the Paphian, not a man's like*
> *Athena, and your cheeks shed a rosy radiance! Well,*
> *since you have a body like that desirous goddess, why*
> *not be queen of marriage as well as Kythereia*
> *(Cytherea) with her wealth of fine hair, and receive a*
> *bridegroom into your chamber? If it please you, leave*
> *Athena and sleep with Hermes and Ares. If it please*
> *you, take up the bow and arrows of the Erotes (Loves),*
> *if your passion is so strong for a quiver full of arrows. I*
> *ask pardon of your beauty, but I am much better than*
> *you. See what a vigorous body I have! Look at Aura's*

---

357 Diodorus Siculus 5.2.3.
358 Homeric Hymn 2 to Demeter.
359 Dionysiaca 48.302.

> *body like a boy's, and her step swifter than Zephyros*
> *(the West Wind)! See the muscles upon my arms, look*
> *at my breasts, round and unripe, not unlike a woman.*
> *You might almost say that yours are swelling with*
> *drops of milk! Why are your arms so tender, why are*
> *your breasts not round like Aura's, to tell the world*
> *themselves of unviolated maidenhood?"* [360]

An outraged Artemis complains to Nemesis, the goddess of vengeance, about Aura insulting her body and requests that Nemesis take revenge. Nemesis replied by telling Artemis that she would see Aura in a mountain stream weeping for her lost virginity.[361]

Aura is violated by the god Dionysus while in a deep sleep. When she wakes up and realises what happened, she goes on a killing spree. As her pregnancy becomes more visible, Artemis taunts her, returning the derisions that Aura had previously directed at her. Her revenge is complete when Artemis delays attending to Aura when she is in labour, ensuring that Aura has a painful childbirth. Aura then births twins - she devours one child, and Artemis intervenes by taking the other and giving it to his father, Dionysus, to look after. Aura continues to be frantic about her predicament and commits suicide by jumping into a river.[362]

## ARTEMIS & BASTET

In the writings of Herodotus, we find Artemis equated with the Egyptian cat-headed goddess Bastet. In his description of frequent assemblies held in Boubastis, the cult centre for the Bastet, he recounts that there are ceremonies for Artemis.[363] He described the city of Buto as the centre for a great Egyptian oracle, saying that there was a temple of Apollo and Artemis (equated here to the Egyptian deities Horus and Bastet).[364] Herodotus also identifies Dionysus with Osiris and Demeter with Isis, and says that this is

---

360 Dionysiaca 48.302.
361 Dionysiaca 48.375.
362 Dionysiaca 48.848.
363 Herodotus 2.59.
364 Herodotus 2.155.

where the poet Aiskhylos came up with the idea that Artemis was the daughter of Demeter.³⁶⁵

Herodotus was practising *interpretatio graeca*, a process through which foreign deities were translated into their Greek counterparts based on perceived similarities in their appearance or function.

It is interesting to note that the monster Typhon attacks the Olympian gods in the Metamorphoses. The gods who fled to Egypt changed into animal forms to hide, and in this story Artemis assumed the form of a cat.³⁶⁶

## ARTEMIS & BENDIS

The Thracian goddess Bendis was known to the Greeks by the 6th century BCE, mentioned in a fragment by Hipponax.³⁶⁷ She was later called two-speared in the comedy *The Thracian Women by Cratinus* in 442 BCE.³⁶⁸ This is significant as Artemis was sometimes depicted carrying two hunting spears.

> "They [the Thracians] worship no gods but Ares,
> Dionysus, and Artemis [Ares, Sabazios and Bendis].
> Their princes ... worship Hermes [Zalmoxis]." ³⁶⁹

There is little recorded information about Bendis, though Herodotus mentions Thracian and Paionian women having straw with them when they sacrificed to Artemis Basileis (royal) [i.e. Bendis].³⁷⁰

Plato also mentions Artemis and Bendis as equated in *The Republic*, saying, *"Bendis, the Thracian Artemis".*³⁷¹

## ARTEMIS, BRITOMARTIS & DIKTYNNA

As mentioned several times, Artemis was conflated with the Cretan Britomartis and Diktynna. Both their names and titles were

---

365 Herodotus 2.156.
366 Antoninus Liberalis, Metamorphoses 28; Ovid, Metamorphoses 5.319.
367 Hipponax fragment 127 in Les fragments du poète Hiponnax – O. Masson, 1962.
368 Fragment 85 in Poetae Comici Graeci – R Kassel & C. Austin, 1983.
369 Herodotus 5.7.
370 Herodotus 4.33.
371 Plato, The Republic, Book 1.

shared with Artemis, and by the 5th century BCE, these goddesses had largely been assimilated into Artemis.[372]

*"They [the Spartans] surname her [Artemis] also Limnaie [Lady of the Lake], though she is not really Artemis but Britomartis of Crete."*[373]

Apuleius mentions Artemis, describing herself as *"Dictynna Diana to the arrowbearing Cretans."* [374] This title is also used in the Orphic Hymns, where she was described as a *"torch-bearing Goddess, Diktynna divine"*. [375]

Britomartis was said to have been born at Kaino in Crete as the daughter of Zeus and Carme. This may indicate that they are half-sisters, sharing Zeus as their father. Britomaris invented the hunting nets (diktya) from which she took her name and was seen in earlier times as a hunting companion of Artemis.[376]

The hill on Crete from which Britomartis leapt to escape the attentions of King Minos was called Diktaion (hill of nets), and altars were set up there to sacrifice to her. Callimachus states that the garlands worn were pine or mastic but never myrtle.[377]

# ARTEMIS & DIONYSUS

After Leto and Apollo, Dionysus seems to be the deity most frequently associated with Artemis. Artemis fights on his side in the Indian Wars of Dionysus and works hard at trying to help him when Hera sends him mad.[378]

It is not surprising that there was a strong bond between Artemis, a goddess of the wilds who was worshipped by women, and Dionysus, a god of the wilds also worshipped by women. Dionysus was moreover a son of Zeus and, as such, a half-brother to Artemis. He would, on occasion, hunt with her.[379] Pindar describes Artemis

---

372 Cretan Cults and Festivals – R.F. Willetts, p183, 1962.
373 Pausanias 3.14.2.
374 Apuleius 11.5.
375 Orphic Hymn 36 to Artemis.
376 Diodorus Siculus 5.76.3.
377 Callimachus, Hymn 3 to Artemis.
378 See e.g. Dionysiaca 32.100, 36.28.
379 Dionysiaca 44.198

yoking savage lions for Dionysus.[380] In an early version of the tale of Theseus, Artemis killed Ariadne for having been unfaithful to Dionysus at his request.[381]

As with Zeus, Artemis seems to bear Dionysus no ill will when he rapes her attendant nymphs, which include the Titan Aura and the nymph Nikaia.

A later myth Servius recounts depicts Dionysus turning Karya, the daughter of King Dion of Lacedaemon, into a nut tree. Artemis told the Laconians what had happened, and they founded the sanctuary for her there as Artemis *Karyatis, of the walnut tree*.[382]

## ARTEMIS & HEKATE

Apollodorus wrote that the birthplace of Artemis was Delos, formerly known as *Asteria*[383], named after Asteria, the mother of Hekate and sister of Leto. In the most popular accounts, Artemis is the cousin of Hekate, and their mothers, Asteria and Leto, are sisters. However, Euripides refers to Hekate as a daughter of Leto, making an even stronger connection to Artemis.[384]

> "O Artemis, Who, too, were once <u>protectress</u>, mighty one, Mistress, <u>who burst forth from the earth</u>, <u>dog-leader</u>, <u>All-tamer</u>, <u>crossroad goddess</u>, triple-headed, <u>Bringer of light</u>, august <u>virgin</u>, I call you <u>Fawn-slayer</u>, crafty, O <u>infernal one</u>, And many-formed."[385]

This love spell from the Greek Magical Papyri (PGM), which starts with an offering to Selene, shows how the titles and attributes of Artemis and Hekate were frequently shared, as all the attributes underlined in the quote above could be attributed to both these goddesses.

---

380 Pindar Dithyrambs: Heracles the Bold.
381 Odyssey 11.324.
382 Servius, ad Verg. Bucolics 8.29.
383 Apollodorus 1.4.
384 Euripides, Phoi, 109.
385 PGM IV:2721-26.

Both Artemis and Hekate were depicted as beautiful maidens, sometimes in short skirts and hunting boots, and both were at times accompanied by dogs and serpents and with two torches.

*"O Artemis, thou maid divine, Diktynna, huntress,*
*fair to see, O bring that keen-nosed pack of thine, and*
*hunt through all the house with me. O Hecate, with*
*flaming brands."* [386]

Both were also closely associated with childbirth and women's health and reproductive issues.

Pausanias, Hesiod and Lyric fragment 3.215 all refer to Artemis turning Iphigeneia into Hekate. As Iphigeneia is associated with Artemis, the whole connection becomes very tangled.

*"We pray; and that Artemis-Hekate watch*
*over the childbed of their women."* [387]

From about the 5th century BCE, there was a significant degree of association between Artemis and Hekate, with their names even being joined as Artemis-Hekate. Along with sharing epithets such as Enodia, Propylaií, and Phosphorus, it can sometimes become impossible to entirely separate them. Hekate was even named the Chthonian Artemis on occasion.

On the Pergamon Frieze (2nd century BCE), a triple Hekate and Artemis are depicted as separate goddesses, showing the two goddesses battling the giants Klytios and Otios.

## ARTEMIS & HERA

As the daughter of Zeus by Leto, Artemis would never be popular with Hera, as she was a constant reminder of her husband's infidelity. The primary interaction between Hera and Artemis occurred during the two times they fought. Both times, Hera overpowered Artemis and drove her away.

---

386 Aristophanes, Frogs 1358.
387 Aiskhylos, Suppliants, 674-7.

The first occasion is in the Indian Wars of Dionysus when Hera used one of Zeus' clouds as a shield from Artemis' arrows and threw chunks of hail at her, breaking her bow and knocking her over.[388]

Towards the end of the Trojan War, the Olympian gods started fighting each other. Artemis criticized her brother Apollo for refusing to fight the sea god Poseidon after he boasted that he could beat him. Apollo remained quiet throughout, saying nothing to his sister, but Hera, who overheard Artemis, rebuked her, challenging her to do better. Artemis, who, as before in the Indian Wars, stood against Hera, found herself being challenged by the queen of the gods. Hera hit Artemis, sending her bow and arrows flying. Artemis ran away crying while her mother, Leto, picked up her bow and arrows behind her and went looking for her. Artemis had already run to Zeus and complained to him that Hera hit her.[389]

The other instance of Artemis and Hera together occurred when they were attacked by the Aloadai giants. Artemis caused the giants to kill each other by shapeshifting into a deer and running between them. In the confusion, they speared one another. On that occasion, Artemis saved Hera from being attacked, demonstrating that not all interactions between these goddesses were hostile.

## ARTEMIS & HERAKLES

The paths of Artemis and Herakles seem to cross frequently in the Greek myths. The third of his twelve labours was to capture the Cerityneanm Hind, sister to the four deer that pulled Artemis' chariot. He managed to wound and catch the creature but then was met by an angry Artemis and Apollo. Herakles explained the reason for his actions to the twins. In turn, Artemis healed the hind and allowed Hercules to continue.

His sixth labour was to kill and drive off the Stymphalian birds, which he did with a bow and arrow after using bronze clappers made by Hephaestus to scare the birds. There was a temple of Artemis Stymphalia at Stymphalos, which had carvings of the Stymphalian

---

388 Dionysiaca 36.28.
389 Iliad 21.470.

birds, suggesting a link to the birds. There is no record of Artemis being upset by Herakles on this occasion.[390]

Callimachus recounts that when she entered Olympus, Herakles challenged Artemis to shoot boars and oxen rather than deer and hares, as the latter did no harm.[391] However, in the same text, Callimachus also mentions the other gods laughing at Herakles for his gluttony, as he had the task of bringing in the game that Artemis had killed.

Artemis and Herakles both also play a role in the story of Prometheus. After Artemis, Apollo, and Leto persuaded Zeus to release the Titan god Prometheus from his bondage, Herakles was sent to free and bring Prometheus back.[392]

## ARTEMIS & LETO

According to Homer, Leto was the daughter of the Titan gods Coeus and Phoebe. She was the mother of the twins and sister to Asteria. Artemis and Leto have a close relationship. Immediately upon her birth, Artemis helps her mother deliver Apollo, a difficult birth unlike hers. In depictions on vases and friezes, Artemis and Leto are often shown close to each other.

Artemis was vigorous in defending her mother and would kill anyone who threatened or impugned her. At Leto's request, Artemis killed the daughters of Queen Niobe. With Apollo, she killed the giant Tityos, who had tried to molest Leto. She also killed the Python with Apollo for chasing Leto when she was pregnant and many rulers for refusing Leto sanctuary at Delphi.

Leto looked after Artemis like a good mother. When Artemis returned to Olympus, Leto was described as covering Artemis' shoulders, trimming her disordered hair, pulling down her robe and arranging her bow and arrows.[393]

---

390 Pausanias 8.22.7.
391 Callimachus, Hymn 3 to Artemis.
392 Valerius Flaccus, Argonautica 4.60.
393 Achilleid 1.344.

When Artemis fled to Zeus after being hit by Hera, Leto retrieved her bow and arrows.[394] Leto was also described as having her *"heart beat happily"* when Artemis and her nymphs gathered to play.[395]

## ARTEMIS & NEMESIS

Artemis and Nemesis were depicted as winged, virginal and vengeful goddesses. *The Suidas* goes so far as to equate Artemis and Nemesis, claiming that the 3rd century BCE writer Demetrios of Skepsis said this.[396] However, note that Suidas was written in the 10th century CE, during the Byzantine era.

In the Dionysiaca, Artemis asks Nemesis for her aid in punishing the Titan Aura for abusing her. Aura stroked her breasts and commented on their fullness, saying that her own body was much better, being more muscular.[397] Artemis asked Nemesis to turn Aura into stone, but Nemesis declined, pointing out that she was also a Titan. Instead, she promises to make Aura lose her highly prized virginity.[398]

## ARTEMIS & PAN

Pan gifted Artemis a pack of hunting dogs; both Artemis and Pan are deities associated with the wilderness.

As with other gods, when Pan tries to molest her nymphs, Artemis does not get angry with him, although, on at least one occasion, she was described as complaining when Pan chased her nymphs.[399]

Pausanias refers to a sanctuary of Asclepius at Sikyon, where there was an image of Pan sitting on one side of the enclosure and one of Artemis standing on the other side.[400]

---

394 Iliad 21.470.
395 Odyssey 6.102.6.
396 Suidas, Arasteia
397 Dionysiaca 48.351-69.
398 Dionysiaca 48.470-3.
399 Silvae 2.3.1.
400 Pausanias 2.10.2-3.

## ARTEMIS & SELENE

> *"Chrysippus in his Old Physics, shows that Artemis is Selene and credits it with an influence on childbirth, says that at the full moon not only do women have the easiest labour but all animals have an easy birth."* [401]

Selene, as the Moon Goddess, was frequently identified with Artemis. This occurred regularly from around the 2nd century BCE onwards.[402]

> *"Both Helios and Selene are closely associated with these [Apollo & Artemis], since they are the causes of the temperature of the air. And both pestilential diseases and sudden deaths are imputed to these gods [Apollo & Artemis]."* [403]

## ARTEMIS & ZEUS

> *"It was your wife, Hera of the white arms, who hit me, father, since hatred and fighting have fastened upon the immortals."* [404]

Artemis was one of Zeus' favourite children. Callimachus describes the young Artemis sitting on Zeus' knee and making many demands. Artemis wanted as many names as Apollo, a bow and arrows, eighty nymphs, all the mountains in the world, and a city. Zeus gave her everything she asked for and more, giving her sixty cities and making her guardian over streets and harbours.[405]

In return, Artemis did not seem to bear any ill will to her father when he seduced her attendant nymphs, as was the case for Callisto and Taygete. She was also described as weaving Zeus' robes for him with Athena and Persephone.[406]

---

401 Greek Lyric I Alcaeus Frag 390 (from Scholiast on Iliad).
402 See e.g. Cicero, De Natura Deorum 2.27, 3.19.
403 Strabo 14.1.6.
404 Iliad 21.470.
405 Callimachus, Hymn 3 to Artemis.
406 Diodorus Siculus 5.2.3.

# 17.
# THE COMPANIONS OF ARTEMIS

Artemis is often shown in myths as having companions, many female – including mortals, goddesses and nymphs. Her companions had almost always taken a vow of chastity, which was sometimes broken, which would lead to the vengeance of one type or another, often resulting in the death or metamorphosis of the companion.

Being a companion to Artemis had its risks. A number of her companions were seduced or raped by gods. Reference to this can be found in the poems of Stratius:

> *"Shall I never keep this unseemly, wanton brood from lustful rapine? Must my chaste band of followers ever grow fewer?"* 407

## ARTEMIS' NYMPHS

Artemis had a wide range of companions. Foremost of these were the eighty nymphs she requested from Zeus as a child. These were the Amnisiades, twenty nymphs who were daughters of the Cretan River god Amninos, and sixty of the (three thousand) Oceanides, sea nymphs. Other nymphs also joined her entourage as she travelled across the lands.

> *"[Artemis to Zeus] 'And give me sixty daughters of Oceanus (Oceanides) for my choir – all nine years old, all maidens yet ungirdled; and give me for handmaidens twenty Nymphs of Amnisos who shall tend well my buskins, and, when I shoot no more at lynx or stag, shall tend my swift hounds."* 408

---

407 Silvae 2.3.1.
408 Callimachus, Hymn 3 to Artemis.

# AMETHYST

Amethyst was a nymph who was transformed into stone by Artemis. Aristotle tells the tale of Amethyst, the unfortunate nymph who encountered Dionysus when he was in a bad mood and had sworn to kill the next mortal he met. Amethyst cried out to Artemis, who transformed her into a white stone. Dionysus felt remorse and poured wine over the stone, turning it purple. From this came the gemstone amethyst, which was thought to protect against drunkenness (amethyst means *not drunk* or *against drunkenness*).

# ANTIKLEIA

The Phocian princess Antikleia, who married Laertes and became the mother of the hero Odysseus, was another favourite companion of Artemis in her maiden youth.[409] When he visited the underworld, Odysseus discovered his mother had died and asked her if Artemis had slain her.[410] Antikleia replies it was not Artemis that killed her but her longing for his company and counsel.

# ARETHOUSA

The Arcadian nymph Arethousa was a companion of Artemis before her transformation into the sacred spring at her shrine in Syracuse, Sicily, to save her from rape by the river god Alpheios.[411]

Pausanias describes a ritual performed at the sanctuary of Artemis Soteira at Aegium, where offering cakes were taken from the sanctuary and thrown into the sea. Priests would declare that they sent the cakes to Arethousa in Syracuse (Syracuse, Sicily).[412] Aelian mentions a tame sacred eel in the spring of Arethousa.[413]

The fountain is still flowing strongly today, just a few paces from the sea on the islet of Ortygia, a small rocky island connected by a bridge to the rest of the modern city of Syracuse. Today a

---

409 Callimachus, Hymn 3 to Artemis.
410 Odyssey, 11.172.
411 Ovid, Metamorphoses 5.610, Pausanias 5.7.2.
412 Pausanias, 7.24.3.
413 Aelian, On Animals 8.4.

contemporary sculpture of Arethousa being chased by Alpheios stands above it, and the ruins of an impressive Artemision can be found nearby, as well as a temple to Athena (now the Cathedral), as well as the ruins of a temple to Apollo.

# ATALANTA

The Skhoinean princess Atalanta was abandoned in the wilds at the order of her father, King Iasios, who had wanted a son. Artemis pitied the baby girl and sent a she-bear to raise her. As she grew up, Artemis taught her the ways of animals, archery, and hunting, and she became the fastest runner in Greece and an excellent hunter. She rejected love and was a dedicated follower of Artemis for many years.[414]

Atalanta, when she was only seventeen, first wounded the Calydonian Boar, allowing the other hunters to finish it off despite their protests at her presence on the hunt. Some versions of the myth have the fighting after the boar's death started by Meleagros giving the skin to Atalanta for first wounding the boar and because he was in love with her.[415]

When her father learned of Atalanta's fame, he implored her to return to him. Embarrassed by his tears, Atalanta agreed to go to the city and learn the ways of civilization. She refused to marry, however, saying she would only marry the man who could outrun her in a race. Any suitor who raced her and lost would be killed. Aphrodite intervened and gave Hippomenes three golden apples from the garden of the Hesperides. During the race, he dropped the apples at different times, distracting Atalanta, who stopped to pick the apples up, losing the race. Through this, Hippomenes could marry Atalanta. Aphrodite, having stolen one of Artemis' maidens, was not content, as the lovers did not thank her. As punishment, she caused them to have sex in a cave sacred to Kybele, who in turn transformed them into lions and yoked them to her chariot to be her steeds.[416]

---

414 Callimachus, Hymn 3 to Artemis.
415 Apollodorus, The Library 1.66.
416 Ovid, Metamorphoses, 10.98.

## BEROE

The goddess Beroe, daughter of Aphrodite and Adonis, hunted with Artemis in her maiden years, carrying the hunting nets.[417] Beroe was wooed by two gods who desired her, Dionysus and Poseidon. Beroe did not want to marry the gods, wishing to remain a maiden instead. However, Zeus intervenes and sets a contest between the two gods for Beroe's hand in marriage. Poseidon won and took her to become his wife.[418]

## BRITOMARTIS

*"Which of the Nymphs dost thou [Artemis] love above the rest ... Beyond others thou lovest the Nymph of Gortyn, Britomartis, slayer of stags, the goodly archer."* [419]

Britomartis is both a goddess and a Cretan girl who is made immortal after jumping into the sea to escape the lustful advances of King Minos. She took refuge with some fishermen who hid her in their nets, which some sources claim is why she was also called Diktynna (meaning she of the nets).

After this, one of the fishermen, Andromedes, attempted to molest her, but she fled into a grove on Aigina and disappeared through the intervention of Artemis. As a result, she was also known as Aphaia (meaning one who disappeared), and a temple was set up in the grove where she vanished.

Britomartis presided over the shrines of her tutelary goddess and rescuer Artemis on the islands of Aigina and Crete.[420]

## CALLISTO

The Arcadian princess Callisto was a hunting companion and close friend of Artemis until Zeus ravished her. Artemis made

---

417 Dionysiaca 41.51.
418 Dionysiaca 41.51f.
419 Callimachus, Hymn 3 to Artemis.
420 Antoninus Liberalis, Metamorphoses 40.

Callisto her chief companion until her molestation at the hands of Zeus.

> *"She touched the goddess' bow: 'this bow I touch,' she cried, 'Be a witness to my virginity.' Artemis praised her, and said: 'Keep the pledge you vowed and you will be my companions' princeps."* [421]

For more information, see Callisto's Fall in chapter 5.

# IPHIGENEIA

Iphigeneia was described as the daughter of King Agamemnon, a princess who was saved by Artemis after she was offered a sacrifice to appease the Goddess due to her father's boasts. Iphigeneia presided over the shrine in Scythian Tauros on the Black Sea.

For more see Goddess of Women, chapter 8.

# KYRENE

Kyrene, alternatively described as a nymph or a Thessalian princess, was a companion of Artemis until her seduction by Apollo.[422] Kyrene killed a lion with her bare hands, showing her strength and prowess.[423] Kyrene was another beloved companion whom Artemis gave two hunting dogs before her seduction.[424]

# MUSES

Although primarily attendants of Apollo, the nine Muses were also occasional companions of Artemis.[425] Artemis also joined them in singing and dancing, two activities they inspired most.[426]

---

421 Ovid, Fasti 2.155.
422 Apollonius Rhodius, Argonautica 2.498.
423 Dionysiaca 25.180.
424 Callimachus, Hymn 3 to Artemis.
425 Homeric Hymn 27 to Artemis.
426 Homeric Hymn 3 to Pythian Apollo.

# NIKAIA

The Phrygian nymph Nikaia was a companion of Artemis, who killed Hymnus, a shepherd who obsessively pursued her by shooting him with her bow. She was a nymph associated with a river and lake in north-west Anatolia.

Eros, the god of erotic love, was angered by her killing of Hymnus and retaliated by causing the god Dionysus to become infatuated with her, molesting her while she was sleeping.[427] She is caused to fall asleep by drinking wine or a sleep potion. Around the same time, Dionysus also took as a lover the nymph Aura, daughter of Kybele, who conceived twins by him. Aura went into a frenzy after birthing twins, brutally killing and devouring one. Artemis, horrified at Aura's behaviour, rescues the second, Iacchus, who is given by Dionysus to Nikaia to breastfeed and raise.

Iacchus went on to be received into the Mysteries, honoured alongside his father Dionysus and the god Zagreus, and becoming the God of the joyous ritual cry *Iache!* in the Eleusian mysteries, alongside Demeter, Persephone and Hekate. He is usually depicted as bearing twin torches in the procession.

# PHOLOE

Pholoe, a nymph from central Italy, was a companion of Artemis until she was transformed into a spring to save her from rape at the hands of Pan. Artemis threw (not shot) an arrow at Pholoe, and the arrow's feathers touched her left hand, transforming her.[428]

# PHYLOMONE

Phylomone, another Arcadian princess, was a hunting companion of Artemis until her seduction by the war god Ares in the guise of a shepherd.[429]

---

427 Dionysiaca 16.392.
428 Silvae 2.3.1.
429 Plutarch, Greek & Roman Parallel Stories 36.

# PLEIADES

The Pleiades (doves) were the seven daughters of the Titan Atlas and the nymph Pleione. They were companions to Artemis and nurses and teachers to the young Dionysus. They were pursued by Orion for seven years[430] and were initially transformed into doves to escape Zeus' attention and then into stars. It was claimed that was why Orion was close to the constellation of the Pleiades, as even then, he still tried to pursue them.[431] Six of the seven Pleiades had sex with gods, and one with a mortal. This was given as the reason why only six of the seven stars in the Pleiades were clearly visible.[432] The eldest of the Pleiades, Maia, was the mother of the Trickster God Hermes by Zeus.

# PROKRIS

The Attican lady Prokris hunted with Artemis before her marriage to Kephalos. When Kephalos abandoned Prokris for the goddess of the dawn Eos, Artemis helped her regain her husband. She gave Prokris a hunting dog that no prey could escape from and a javelin that never missed the mark to give to her husband as gifts to tempt him back, a ploy that worked.[433] A later account has Prokris trying to rejoin Artemis and her followers after her husband was unfaithful, but Artemis sent her away as she was no longer a virgin.[434]

# SYRINX

Syrinx, an Arcadian nymph, was another companion of Artemis, who was said to look very similar to Artemis.[435] Fleeing from the lustful pursuits of the licentious god Pan, who had been encouraged to lust after Syrinx by Aphrodite, who was angered at Syrinx's chastity.[436] She hid in the river Ladon (Southern Greece) reeds and begged the river spirits to transform her into the reeds to

---

430 Hyginus, Astronomica 2.21.
431 Pindar, Odes Nemean 2 str 3.
432 Hyginus, Astronomica 2.21.
433 Callimachus, Hymn 3 to Artemis.
434 Hyginus, Fabulae 189.
435 Ovid, Metamorphoses 1.689.
436 Ovid, Metamorphoses 1.689.

preserve her virginity. Pan cut the reeds during his search for her, then believing that he had accidentally slayed her by cutting the reeds, turned the reeds into his panflutes so that he could keep her forever close.[437] The Ancient Greek name for panflutes was Syrinx.

---

437 Dionysiaca 42.363.

# 18.
# TEMPLE ATTENDANTS

Several companions or attendants of Artemis became guardians of specific temples.

## BIRD-LEGGED NYMPHS

Bird-legged nymphs were said to attend the Stymphalian shrine of Artemis in Arcadia in southern Greece.[438]

## ASPALIS

Artemis granted some maidens immortality so they could eternally guard her shrines. She granted a girl called Aspalis immortality after she hung herself before her wedding to preserve her virginity, and she became the guardian spirit of Artemis' shrine in Melite in northern Greece.

## HEKAERGE, LOXO & OUPIS

She also made three Hyperborean maidens called Hekaerge, Loxo and Oupis immortal to be attendants of her shrine on her birth island of Delos. Different sources refer to these maidens, including Callimachus, who declares they were all the daughters of Boreas, the North Wind.[439]

They are also mentioned by Nonnus[440], and Hekaerge and Oupis are mentioned by Pausanias when referring to Delos.[441]

---

438 Pausanias 8.22.4.
439 Callimachus, Hymn 4 to Delos, 292.
440 Dionysiaca 48.302, 48.330 and 5.480.
441 Pausanias 1.43.4, 5.7.8.

## PHYLONOE

A Spartan princess called Phylonoe (alternatively called Polyboia) was made immortal by Artemis and charged to watch over her Spartan shrines.[442]

## HEMITHEA & PARTHENOS

Two other princesses, Hemithea and Parthenos, from the island of Naxos, were immortalized by Apollo. They became the attendant spirits at the shrines of Artemis at Bubastos and Kastabos.

## KATARIA-EUKLEIA

Artemis also sometimes rewarded women who had demonstrated selfless behaviour. A Theban Lady called Makaria-Eukleia, who sacrificed herself to save her family and died a virgin, was immortalised to look after the shrines of Boiotia in southern Greece.[443]

## HIPPOLYTUS

The Troizenoan prince Hippolytus, a male companion of Artemis, was slain through the wiles of Aphrodite. The god of healing, Asclepius, brought Hippolytus back to life. At this point, Artemis (as Diana) made him the attendant of her Arician shrine in Nemi, Italy.[444] Euripides recounts this tale in great detail in his play *Hippolytus*.

## MEGABYZOI, EUNUCH PRIESTS

According to Strabo, there were eunuch priests who served Artemis at Ephesus, which he said were called the Megabyzoi. These individuals, also named Megabyxos, may have come from different backgrounds or may have been from a Persian royal bloodline. The name means *he who serves god / the divine*.

---

442 Pausanias 3.19.4 and Apollodorus 3.126.
443 Plutarch, Aristides 20.5.
444 Pausanias 2.27.4.

Eunuch priests at the Ephesian temple would not have been unusual for the region, especially as the name Artemis became used for older indigenous mother goddesses there.

Artemis' cult at Ephesus is closely linked to that of Kybele, the daughter of the Phrygian Sky God and Earth Goddess, who was born as Agdistis, a hermaphrodite, who was castrated by the gods and became Kybele. She was closely identified with the Mountain Mother, Mother of the Gods, Great Mother (Magna Mater) and the goddesses Rhea and Hekate – and with Artemis. The gods, out of fear for Agdistis' power, castrated Agdistis, and where his penis fell to the ground, an almond tree sprouted. The seed of this tree was consumed by the daughter of the river god Saggarios, who became pregnant and birthed Attis. She left the baby exposed to the elements to die, but a he-goat raised the child. The child had an otherworldly beauty, and when Kybele saw him she fell deeply in love with him.

Pausanius recounts that Kybele attended the wedding feast of Attis to a King's daughter. Her presence caused both Attis and the bride's father to castrate themselves.

Attis is equated to the hero Iasion, a lover of Demeter in the mysteries of Samothrace and the father of the Cretan Plutus, a blind god of wealth who distributes wealth equally to humans.

It is interesting to note that eunuch priests were found throughout the Anatolian region, serving at the temples of Artemis, Kybele and Hekate.

# 19.
# ARTEMIS & MEN

Artemis was closely associated with women, particularly the protection of young girls and the transition into adulthood and marriage, as well as the difficulties of pregnancy and birthing. However, Artemis had many male worshippers; men attended her temples and shrines and honoured her. Men also served as priests in her temples.

With the frequent references to Artemis in association with war and celebrations of battles, it is demonstrably apparent that Artemis was honoured by both men and women. Furthermore, Artemis appears to have held a role in the coming-of-age rituals for young men who had to prove their masculinity and strength. These rituals often involved bloodshed, whipping and other forms of violence that may seem barbaric to us today but marked significant moments in the lives of those who participated.

## PRINCE HIPPOLYTUS

The best-known of Artemis' male devotees was Prince Hippolytus of Troizenos, son of Theseus and Queen Hippolyta, discussed in a previous chapter. He dedicated himself to a chaste life as a hunter, worshipping Artemis and being blessed with her company. He was killed through the jealous wiles of Aphrodite for neglecting her, and Artemis persuaded Asclepius to bring him back to life and made him a temple attendant in Aricia.

## ASTRABAKOS & ALOPEKOS

In Sparta during the Roman period, young men had to undergo severe flogging until the altar of Artemis Orthia was smeared with blood. This ritual flogging was known as diamastigosis and was a test of endurance to demonstrate the worthiness of the young would-be warriors. The origins of this ceremony were said to come from the discovery of an image of Artemis Orthia that was lost from a temple and subsequently rediscovered. Two Spartan warriors, Astrabakos and Alopekos, found the statue of Artemis and went insane. After a temple was set up around the statue for her, Artemis was temporarily propitiated. However, during a sacrifice to her, groups of Limnatians, Kynosourians and Mesoans started quarrelling, and in the fight, many were killed at her altar. Artemis, in her wrath, slew the rest through disease.

When they petitioned an oracle, the Spartans were told the only way to appease Artemis was to stain the altar with human blood. At the start, they chose lots and gave Artemis a human sacrifice until the whipping of boys seeking to enter manhood was substituted, ensuring a plentiful supply of blood for the altar.[445] During the scourging, a priestess would hold the light wooden image. The statue was said to become very heavy if the men scourging gave light blows to a boy because of his beauty or rank. The priestess would then chastise the scourgers to ensure the boy was appropriately scourged.

## CHEESE-STEALING RITUALS

Another instance where flogging came into play was the archaic cheese-stealing ritual, quoted by Xenophon.[446] In this, two opposing groups of young men would contest some cheese stored on the altar. The first group defended the cheese with whips, and the second tried to steal it.

## TAUROPOLOS RITES

Euripides refers to a mock sacrifice performed at the temple of Artemis Tauropolos in Attica, where a man would have his neck scratched with a knife so that blood was drawn. It is very tempting to see this as part of an initiatory rite, with the first violent blood being shed in honour of Artemis.

> *"And institute this custom: when the people celebrate,*
> *as atonement for your sacrifice let them hold a sword to*
> *a man's neck and cause blood to flow, for holiness's*
> *sake and that the goddess have due honour."* [447]

---

445 Pausanias 3.16.7.
446 Lakedaimonion Politeia 2.9.
447 Euripides, Iphigeneia in Tauris, 1458-61.

# 20.
# ARTEMIS' SYMBOLS

Artemis, like all the gods, had symbols that were woven into her stories, myths and worship over millennia. These symbols allow us to recognise Artemis and gain a deeper understanding of her roles and functions.

Examples of Artemis' symbols include:

- Bees
- Birds, including partridges, quails, goldfinch, swans etc.
- Bow, Quiver & Arrows
- Golden Chariot
- Herbs & Plants, including Artemesia.
- Hunting Dogs
- Moon
- Silver & Gold
- Spear / Javelin
- Springs & Fountains
- Sword
- Torches
- Wild Animals, including Deer and Bears

Many of these are explored in detail in previous chapters. What follows is information that did not fit neatly into the preceding chapters but which might be of interest to some readers.

## PLANTS & TREES

Several plants and trees are considered sacred or otherwise associated with Artemis. These include:

- Artemisia Herbs, especially Wormwood
- Cedar
- Cypress trees
- Laurel
- Myrtle

- Oak
- Palm
- Poppies
- Walnut

Cypress was sacred to Artemis due to her birth occurring in a grove of cypress trees, though other versions of the myth say she was born under a palm tree. It might be for this reason that temples and sanctuaries for Artemis were often built within cypress groves.[448]

Alternative versions of her birth have it occurring under a palm tree, which was sacred to her mother, Leto.

> *"The old palm tree [of Delos] played midwife*
> *for Leto with her poor little leaves."* [449]

White poppies were said to be significant in the worship of Artemis in Attica, and a group of bronze statuettes of Artemis from Lousoi in Arcadia (c. 470-400 BCE) show her holding a poppy.[450]

The herb mugwort is sometimes referred to as Artemis' herb and is part of a family of herbs that carry her name. In particular, Mugwort (Artemisia vulgaris) and Wormwood (Artemisia absinthium) are used in concoctions to awaken the psychic senses associated with her. Wormwood is also used to make Absinthe, which is said to induce visions of fairies.

> *"Of these worts that we name Artemisia, it is said*
> *that Diana did find them and delivered their powers*
> *and leechdom to Chiron the Centaur, who first from*
> *these worts set forth a leechdom, and he named these*
> *worts from the name of Diana, Artemis, that is*
> *Artemisia."* [451]

Gerrard, however, gives another reason for the name, saying:

> *"Mugwort is called in Latine, Artemisia, which name*
> *it had of Artemisia Queene of Halicarnassus, and wife*

---

448 Strabo 14.1.20.
449 Dionysiaca 27.259.
450 The Light of the Gods – Eva Parisinou, p81, p189 n5.
451 Herbarium of Apuleius.

*of noble Mausolus King of Caria, who adopted it for her owne herbe."* [452]

# TORCHES

*"She [Artemis] will forsake your miseries and will dissolve the deadly pharmaka of pestilence by melting down with her flame-bearing torches, in nightly fire, the kneaded wax figurines, the evil signs of the magos' art."* [453]

Along with Hekate, Artemis is often shown bearing two torches. Artemis is more often shown with long torches, like the Thracian Bendis, than shorter torches which Hekate is more often depicted with. However, this is interchangeable and both goddesses are shown with long and short torches at different times. These images start occurring from the middle of the 5th century BCE and usually show Artemis receiving worshippers or sacrifices.

A late 5th century BCE cup by Aristophanes shows Artemis with her two torches fighting a Titan, accompanied by Zeus with his thunderbolt fighting another Titan.[454] This theme of Artemis with two torches fighting giants is also seen on a late 5th BCE plate at the British Museum.[455]

Three late 4th or early 3rd century BCE votive reliefs from Ekhinos and Delos to Artemis *Lokhia*, possibly representing thanks for successful births, all show Artemis with a long torch. Euripides describes Iphigeneia using torchlight to purify the statue of Artemis from the matricides committed in its presence.[456]

A custom, which was re-instituted for the modern Olympic Games, is that of the torch race. In ancient Greece, torch races, where the winner would light the sacrificial flame with his torch, were practiced in honour of several deities. The best known of these is the goddess Athena, but this also seems to have been the case for

---

452 Gerrard's Herbal, p254.
453 Oracle of Ephesus, quoted in Magic, Religion, and Syncretism at the Oracle of Claros – Z. Várhelyi p16, in Between Magic and Religion, 2001.
454 Staatliche Museum, Berlin, F2531, cat no 7.18.
455 British Museum E701, London.
456 Euripides, Iphigeneia in Tauris, 2:1224-5.

Artemis *Tauropolos*.⁴⁵⁷ Torch-bearing girls are also seen in depictions from the temple of Artemis at Brauron.

---

457 The Light of the Gods – Eva Parisinou, p38.

# BIBLIOGRAPHY

Aelian, On the Characteristics of Animals Books I-V, 1958, Harvard University Press, Harvard

---------- On the Characteristics of Animals Books VI-X, 1958, Harvard University Press, Harvard

---------- On the Characteristics of Animals Books XII-XVII, 1958, Harvard University Press, Harvard

Apuleius , The Golden Ass, 1990, Harvard University Press, Harvard

Asirvatham, S, & Pache, C.O (eds), Between Magic and Religion 2001, Rowman & Littlefield Publishers Inc, Oxford

Athanassakis, A. (trans), Hesiod: Theogony, Works and Days, Shield, 1984, John Hopkins University Press, Baltimore

---------- The Orphic Hymns: Text, Translation and Notes, 1988, Society of Biblical Literature, Atlanta

Austin, Colin (ed), Aristophanes Thesmophoriazusae, 2004, Oxford University Press, Oxford

Avagianou, Aphrodite, Sacred Marriage in the Rituals of Greek Religion, 1991, Peter Lang, Bern

Baugh, S.M. Cult Prostitution in New Testament Ephesus: A Reappraisal, 1999 in Journal of the Evangelical Theological Society, 42.3, 443-60

Betz, Hans Dieter (ed), The Greek Magical Papyri in Translation, 1986, University of Chicago Press, Chicago

Boardman, John, Athenian Black Figure Vases, 1974, Thames & Hudson, London

---------- Greek Sculpture: The Archaic Period, 1978, Thames & Hudson, London

Bonner, C., Studies in Magical Amulets, Chiefly Graeco-Egyptian, 1950, Ann Arbor, Michigan

Brewster, Harry, The River Gods of Greece, 1997, I.B. Tauris & Co. Ltd, London

Burkert, W., Greek Religion, 1987, Harvard University Press, Harvard

Calame, Claude, Choruses of Young Women in Ancient Greece: Their Morphology, Religious Role, and Social Functions, 1997, Rowman & Littlefield Publishers Inc, Maryland

Callimachus, Hymns, Epigrams, Select Fragments, 1988, John Hopkins University Press, Baltimore

Callimachus, Lycophron, Aratus. Hymns and Epigrams. Lycophron: Alexandra. Aratus: Phaenomena, 1921. Translated by A. W. Mair, G. R. Mair. Loeb Classical Library 129. University Press, Cambridge

Campbell, D.A., Greek Lyric: Sappho Alcaeus, 1982, Harvard University Press, Harvard

---------- Greek Lyric III: Stesichorus, Ibycus, Simonides and Others, 1991, Harvard University Press, Harvard

---------- Greek Lyric V: The New School of Poetry and Anonymous Songs and Hymns, 1993, Harvard University Press, Harvard

Carpenter, Rhys, Folk Tale, Fiction and Saga in the Homeric Epics, 1946, University of California Press, Los Angeles

Carter, Jane Burr, The Masks of Ortheia, 1987, in American Journal of Archaeology 91.3:355-384

Cicero, De Natura Deorum, 2003, Cambridge University Press, Cambridge

Clauss, James J. & Johnston, Sarah Iles, Medea, 1997, Princeton University Press, Princeton

Clement, Paul, New Evidence for the Origin of the Iphigeneia Legend, 1934, in L'Antiquité Classique 3:393-409

Clinton, Kevin, Artemis and the Sacrifice of Iphigeneia in Aeschylus' Agamemnon, 1988, in Language and the Tragic Hero, Scholars Press, USA

Colluthus, The Rape of Helen, 1993, Königshausen & Neumann, Germany

Condos, Theony (trans), Star Myths of the Greeks and Romans: A Sourcebook, Containing the Constellations of Pseudo-Erastophenes and the Poetic Astronomy of Hyginus, 1997, Phanes Press, Minnesota

Cook, Arthur Bernard, Zeus: A Study in Ancient Religion (3 volumes), 1914, Cambridge University Press, Cambridge

Deubner, Ludwig, Attische Feste, 1932, Berlin

Dietrich, B.C., The Origins of Greek Religion, 1974, Walter De Gruyter, Berlin

Dowden, Ken, Death and the Maiden: Girls' Initiation Rites in Greek Mythology, 1989, Routledge, London

Fagles, Robert (trans), The Odyssey, 1999, Penguin Books, London

Faraone, Christopher, & Obbink, Dirk (eds), Magika Hiera: Ancient Greek Magic & Religion, 1991, Oxford University Press, Oxford

Farnell, Lewis R., The Cults of the Greek States (5 volumes), 1896, Clarendon Press, Oxford

Fauth, W., Arktos in den griechischen Zauberpapyri, 1984, in Zeitschrift fur Papyrologie und Epigraphik 57

Fitzgerald, Robert (trans), The Aeneid (Virgil), 1990, Vintage, Canada

Flaccus, Voyage of the Argo: The Argonautica of Gaius, Valerius Flaccus, 1999, John Hopkins University Press, Baltimore

Ford, Andrew, The Origins of Criticism: Literary Culture and Poetic Theory in Classical Greece, 2002, Princeton University Press, Princeton

Frazer, J.G. (trans), Apollodorus: The Library, 1960, Harvard University Press, Harvard

Gager, John G., Curse Tablets and Binding Spells from the Ancient World, 1992, Oxford University Press, Oxford

Garrison, Daniel H., Sexual Culture in Ancient Greece, 2000, Univeristy of Oklahoma Press, Oklahoma

Gershenson, Daniel, Apollo the Wolf God, 1991, Institute for the Study of Man, Virginia

Gordon, R.L., Myth, religion and society, 1977, Cambridge University Press, Cambridge

Graf, Fritz, Magic in the Ancient World, 1997, Harvard University Press, Massachusetts

Green, Peter (trans), The Argonautika (Apollonius Rhodius), 1997, University of California Press, California

Habicht, Christian, Pausanias' Guide to Greece, 1998, University of California Press, California

Herodotus, The Histories, 1992, W.W. Norton & Co, New York

Hesiod, The Homeric Hymns and Homerica, 1981, Harvard University Press, Harvard

Hopfner, T., Hekate-Selene-Artemis und Verwandte in den griechischen Zauberpapyri und auf den Fluchtafeln, Piscicul, Festschrift F.J.Dolger

Hughes, Dennis D., Human Sacrifice in Ancient Greece, 1991, Routledge, London

Hull, D.B., Hounds and Hunting in Ancient Greece, 1964, University of Chicago Press, Chicago

Johnson, Buffie, Lady of the Beasts, 1994, Inner Traditions International, Vermont

Johnston, Sarah Iles, Hekate Soteira, 1990, Scholars Press, Georgia

Kahil, L., Autour de l'Artemis Attique, 1965, in Antike Kunst 8:20-33

----------- L'Artemis de Brauron: rites et mystere, 1977, in Antike Kunst 20:86-98

----------- Artemis, 1984, in Lexicon iconographicum mythologiae classicae 2:618-753

Kassel, R., & Austin, C., Poetae Comici Graeci, 1983, Walter De Gruyter Inc, New York

Kerényi, C., Zeus and Hera, 1975, Routledge & Kegan Paul, London

----------- The Gods of the Greeks, 1951, Thames & Hudson, London

Larson, Jennifer, Greek Heroine Cults, 1995, University of Wisconsin Press, Madison

Lattimore, Richard (trans), The Iliad of Homer, 1961, University of Chicago Press, Chicago

----------- (trans), The Odes of Pindar, 1976, University of Chicago Press, Chicago

----------- (trans), Four Plays by Aristophanes: The Birds, The Clouds, The Frogs, Lysistrata, 1984, Plume, USA

----------- (trans), Iphigeneia in Taurus (Euripides), 1992, Oxford University Press, Oxford

Leslie, Shane, The Greek Anthology, 1929, Ernest Benn Ltd, London

Letharby, W.R., The Earlier Temple of Artemis at Ephesus, 1917, Journal of Hellenic Studies, 37:1-16

Liberalis Antoninus, Metamorphoses, 1992, Routledge, London

Lloyd-Jones, P.H.J., Artemis and Iphigeneia, 1983, in The Journal of Hellenic Studies 103:87-102

Lombardo, S. (trans), Callimachus: Hymns, Epigrams, Select Fragments, 1988, John Hopkins University Press, Baltimore

Lonsdale, Steven H., Dance and Ritual Play in Greek Religion, 1993, John Hopkins University Press, Baltimore

Luck, George, Arcana Mundi: Magic and the Occult in the Greek and Roman Worlds, 1995, John Hopkins University Press, Baltimore

Marinatos, Nannó, The Goddess and the Warrior: The Naked Goddess and Mistress of Animals in Early Greek Religion, 2000, Routledge, London

Marshall, Peter, Hyginus: Fabulae, 2002, K.G. Saur Verlag, Germany

Masson, O., Les fragments du poète Hiponnax, 1962, Paris

Moon, Warren G., Ancient Greek Art and Iconography, 1983, University of Wisconsin Press, Wisconsin

Murphy, Trevor (trans), Pliny the Elder's Natural History, 2004, Oxford University Press, Oxford

Nilsson, Martin P., The Minoan-Mycenaean Religion and its Survival in Greek Religion, 1927, Humphrey Milford, London

----------- Homer and Mycenae, 1933, Methuen & Co Ltd, London

Nonnos, Dionysiaca Books I-XV, 1965, Harvard University Press, Harvard

----------- Dionysiaca Books XVI-XXXV, 1965, Harvard University Press, Harvard

----------- Dionysiaca Books XXXVI-XLVIII, 1966, Harvard University Press, Harvard

Oppian, Cynergetica

Ovid, Metamorphoses, 1998, Oxford University Press, Oxford

----------- Fasti, 2000, Penguin Books, London

Parisinou, Eva, The Light of the Gods: The Role of Light in Archaic and Classical Greek Cult, 2000, Gerald Duckworth & Co Lotd, London

Parke, H.W., Festivals of the Athenians, 1977, London

Perlman, Paula, Acting the She-Bear for Artemis, 1989, in Arethousa Vol 22 no.2.

Philostratus, The Life of Apollonius of Tyana, 1912, Harvard University Press, Harvard

Pindar, The Odes and Selected Fragments, 1998, Everyman, London

Plutarch, Lives (2 volumes), 2001, Modern Library, London

----------- Moralia: Roman Questions, Greek Questions, Greek and Roman Parallel Stories, 1936, Harvard University Press, Harvard

Price, T.H., Kourotrophos: Cults and Representations of the Greek Nursing Deities, 1978, E.J. Brill, Leiden

Quintus Smyrnaeus, The Fall of Troy, 1962, Harvard University Press

Rehm, Rush, Marriage to Death: The Conflation of Wedding and Funeral Rituals in Greek Tragedy, 1994, Princeton University Press, New Jersey

Rouse, W.H.D., Nonnus Dionysiaca Books 1-48 (3 volumes), 1960, Harvard University Press, Cambridge

Harvard, von Rudloff, Robert, Hekate in Ancient Greek Religion, 1999, Horned Owl Publishing, Victoria

Sale, William, The Temple Legends of Arkteia, 1975, in Rheinisches Museum für Philologie Volume 1:265-84.

Schefold, Karl, Myth and Legend in Early Greek Art, 1966, Thames & Hudson, London

Scheid, John, The Craft of Zeus: Myths of Weaving Harvard University Press, Massachusetts

Seltman, Charles, Greek Coins, 1933, Methuen & Co. Ltd, London

Siculus Diodorus, Books I-II, 1985, Harvard University Press, Harvard

----------- Books IV-VIII, 1939, Harvard University Press, Harvard

----------- Books IX-XII, 1939, Harvard University Press, Harvard

----------- Books XVIII-XIX, 1947, Harvard University Press, Harvard

Siebourg, M., Zu den Ephesia Grammata, 1915, in Archiv fur Papyrusforschung 18:594

Simon, Erica, Festivals of Attica, 1983, University of Wisconsin Press, Wisconsin

Simpson, Michael (trans), Gods and Heroes of the Greeks: The Library of Apollodorus, 1976, University of Massachusetts Press, Amherst

Statius, The Thebaid: Seven Against Thebes, 2004, John Hopkins University Press, Baltimore

----------- Silvae, 2003, Harvard University Press, Harvard

----------- Achilleid, 2005, Bristol Phoenix Press, Bristol

Strabo, The Geography of Strabo, 1967, Harvard University Press, Harvard

Swinburne, Algernon Charles, Swinburne's Collected Poetical Works (2 volumes), 1924, William Heinemann, London

Theognis, Elegies of Theognis: A Revised Text Based on a New Collation of the Mutininensis MS, 1979, Ayer Co Publishers, New Hampshire

Thomson, G., The Greek Calendar, 1943, Journal of Hellenic Studies, 63:52-65

Vernant, Jean-Pierre, Myth & Society in Ancient Greece, 1980, Harvester Press Ltd, Brighton

West, M.L., The Hesiodic Catalogue of Women, 1985, Clarendon Press, Oxford

Whalley, Joyce (trans), Pliny the Elder, Historia Naturalis, 1982, Victoria & Albert Museum, London

Willetts, R.F., Cretan Cults and Festivals, 1962, Routledge & Kegan Paul Ltd, London

Xenophon, Die Verfassung Der Spartaner. Lakedaimonion Politeia, 1998, Wissenschaftliche Buchgesellschaft, Hesse

Yavis, C.G., Greek Altars: Origins and Typology, 1949, Saint Louis University Press, Missouri

**Websites**

Perseus Digital Library Project. Ed. Gregory R. Crane, Tufts University. January 2005, <http://www.perseus.tufts.edu>.

Theoi Project. Ed. Aaron Atsma, January 2005, http://www.theoi.com

Latantius, The Divine Institutes, Translated by William Fletcher. From Ante-Nicene Fathers, Vol. 7. Edited by Alexander Roberts, James Donaldson, and A. Cleveland Coxe. (Buffalo, NY: Christian Literature Publishing Co., 1886.) Revised and edited for New Advent by Kevin Knight. <http://www.newadvent.org/fathers/0701.htm>.

# INDEX

Absinthe..................163
Achelous..................62
Achilleid..................23, 146
Acragas..................108
Acropolis..................44
Actaeon..................128, 132
Adamantine..................105
Admetos..................115
Adonis..................108, 128, 152
Adrasteia..................64
Adrasteia..................49, 64
Adrastos..................64
Aegina..................65, 87
Aegium..................123, 150
Aelian..24, 82, 105, 106, 112, 120, 123, 150
Aeneid..................23
Aeschylus..................59, 113
Agamemnon 16, 44, 58, 59, 76, 79, 100, 102, 113, 153, 167
Agesilaus..................125
Agoraia..................64
Agrotera..................52, 65, 103, 138
Aidoios Parthenos..................92
Aigaion..................125
Aigeira..................48
Aigina..................48, 152
Aiginaii..................65, 125
Aigion..................48
Aiskhylos..................25, 141, 144
Aithopia..................65, 135
Aitolí..................66
Aitolia..................66, 78, 106
Akakesion..................48
Akhilleus..................89
Alagonia..................48
Alea..................43, 48
Alexander The Great..................36, 37
Alkathoos..................65, 103
Alkman..................118
Aloadai Giants..................56, 109, 145
Alopekos..................89, 160
Alpheiaia..................66
Alpheios..................66, 95, 123, 150, 151
Alyattes..................52
Amarynthos..................48, 66, 76, 125
Amarysii..................66
Amazons 36, 68, 79, 121, 125, 126, 129, 138
Ameilikhos..................130
Amethyst..................96, 150
Amninos..................149
Amnisiades..................149
Amnisos..................99, 149
Amphictyonic Oath..................138
Amphion..................61
Amphiphontes..................54, 135
Amphissa..................48, 82
Amyklai..................48

Amyklas..................61
Anaeitis..................66
Anahita..................34, 66
Anatolia 16, 17, 35, 36, 42, 64, 68, 80, 83, 154
Androklos..................36
Andromedes..................152
Anethesterion..................50
Ankaios..................108
Anonos..................69
Antheia..................120
Antikleia..................150
Antikyra..................48
Antipater..................20
Antoninus Liberalis 24, 58, 59, 89, 104, 108, 141, 152
Apankhomení..................67, 77
*Apasa*..................35, 36
Apatourion..................50
*Aphaea*..................65
Aphaia..................87, 152
Aphrodite 46, 47, 62, 94, 96, 98, 103, 104, 107, 108, 118, 121, 128, 136, 137, 139, 151, 152, 155, 158, 160, 166
Apollo 14, 15, 16, 25, 26, 27, 29, 30, 31, 32, 36, 48, 52, 53, 55, 56, 57, 61, 63, 65, 66, 73, 76, 77, 78, 80, 89, 90, 98, 103, 106, 107, 109, 113, 114, 115, 116, 117, 118, 119, 127, 129, 130, 131, 133, 135, 137, 138, 140, 142, 145, 146, 148, 151, 153, 158, 163,167
Apollodorus 23, 25, 56, 57, 59, 60, 62, 98, 102, 110, 115, 125, 128, 131, 132, 136, 143, 151, 158
Apollonius Rhodius..................23
Apuleius..................24, 142, 163
Arasteia..................147
Arcadia 43, 48, 51, 60, 71, 72, 75, 76, 79, 82, 83, 84, 85, 87, 108, 115, 157, 163
Archaic..................16, 166, 169
Archer..................115, 116
Archery..................20, 88, 94, 101, 151
Aregon..................66
Ares 52, 56, 125, 126, 134, 138, 139, 141, 154
Aresion..................50
Arethousa 7, 30, 31, 95, 96, 112, 123, 150, 151, 169
Arge..................57
Argolis..................51, 73, 77, 82, 84, 109
Argonautica..................23, 124, 146, 153
Argos..................48, 61, 80
Ariadne..................57, 131, 143
Aricia..................96
Aristarchus..................38
Aristarkha..................43
Ariste..................67, 74
Aristiboule..................67
Aristides..................71, 158

Aristodemos .................................................. 83
Aristomelidas ..................................... 72, 128
Aristomenes ...................................... 121, 122
Aristophanes 23, 46, 69, 76, 86, 89, 94, 95, 101, 106, 144, 164, 166, 168
Arkas ............................................................... 60
Arktoi ............................................................. 47
Arktos ..................................................... 104, 105
Arrows 20, 58, 61, 63, 73, 74, 88, 91, 92, 94, 101, 121, 125, 129, 130, 131, 133, 145, 146, 148, 162
Artemesia ....................................................... 162
Artemis ........................................................... 46
Artemis Of Ephesus ....................................... 78
Artemis Tauropolos ..................................... 161, 165
Artemis-Hekate .................................... 54, 144
Artemision .................. 31, 48, 50, 125, 151
Artemis-Selene ........................................... 132
Asclepius 27, 90, 96, 118, 119, 129, 147, 158, 160
Asherah ........................................................ 118
Asia Minor ......... 16, 17, 37, 42, 62, 85, 136
Aspalis ..................................................... 67, 157
Asphodel ........................................................ 27
Assyria ............................................................ 42
Asteria 15, 27, 28, 32, 90, 106, 135, 143, 146
Astrabakos ............................................. 89, 160
Astrateia ......................................................... 68
Astronomica ........................................ 24, 63, 155
Astronomy .............................................. 23, 60
Astyra ..................................................... 49, 68
Astyrini ........................................................... 68
Atalanta ................................................ 123, 136, 151
Athena 30, 84, 86, 94, 122, 136, 138, 139, 148, 151, 164
Athena Cynthia ............................................. 86
Athenaios ............................................... 54, 135
Athens 36, 43, 44, 48, 50, 65, 67, 74, 78, 79, 126
Athmonia ....................................................... 48
Atlas ............................................................. 155
Attic Calendar ............................................... 50
Attica ....... 26, 43, 53, 79, 104, 161, 163, 170
Aulis ........................................................ 48, 118
Aura ............. 21, 100, 139, 140, 143, 147, 154
Aureliopos ................................................... 115
Azanian Hills ........................................... 48, 77
Baetylic ........................................................... 40
Bargylia .................................................... 49, 75
Basileis ..................................................... 68, 141
Bastet ........................................................... 140
Bay Tree ......................................................... 51
Bear .. 43, 44, 46, 54, 60, 104, 105, 151, 169
Bees ........................................ 19, 39, 40, 41, 42, 162
Bellona ........................................................... 85
Bendis .......................................................... 141
Beroe ............................................................ 152
Birth ............................................................... 28
Blood .................................................... 160, 161
Boar 36, 54, 101, 104, 108, 112, 128, 136, 151
Boedromion ............................................ 50, 52
Boiai ................................................. 48, 84, 113
Boiotia .......................................................... 158
Boreas ................................................ 27, 87, 157
Bosporus Strait ............................................. 80
Boubastis ..................................................... 140
Boulis ............................................................. 48
Bouphagos .................................................. 128
Bouphonion .................................................. 50
Bouto ........................................................... 140
Bow 6, 20, 58, 65, 101, 102, 118, 119, 121, 126, 133, 145, 146, 147, 148, 153, 154, 162
Brauron 34, 43, 44, 45, 46, 47, 48, 51, 59, 69, 85, 104, 119, 121, 165, 168
Brauronia .................... 43, 44, 45, 46, 51, 69
Breasts ........................................................... 21
Britomartis ..................... 78, 141, 142, 152
Bromia ........................................................... 86
Bromios ......................................................... 86
Bronze Age ............................................. 34, 44
Broteas ......................................................... 102
Bubastos ............................................... 49, 158
Bull ........................................................ 59, 109
Buzzard ................................................ 104, 106
Byblos .......................................................... 118
Byzantion ............................................... 49, 80
Caino ............................................................ 142
Cakes ........................................ 52, 54, 110, 123, 150
Calendar ........................................................ 50
Callimachus 23, 27, 28, 29, 32, 61, 71, 76, 77, 80, 87, 88, 89, 90, 91, 92, 94, 99, 101, 102, 110, 119, 120, 121, 124, 126, 127, 128, 129, 133, 134, 135, 137, 142, 146, 148, 149, 150, 151, 152, 153, 155, 157, 166, 168
Callisto .................................... 60, 133, 148, 152
Calydon ................................................ 48, 78, 108
Calydonian Boar ................................. 108, 151
Capua ............................................................ 49
Caryatid ......................................................... 74
Cassius Dio .................................................... 85
Cat ................................................................ 141
Catalogues Of Women .................................. 60
Cedar ...................................................... 74, 162
Cerityneαn Hind .................................. 110, 145
Chalcis ......................................................... 118
Chariot ................. 53, 110, 115, 133, 139, 145
Charisteria .................................... 51, 52, 138
Cheese .......................................................... 161
Chersiphon .................................................... 36
Childbirth 11, 12, 15, 31, 45, 46, 58, 69, 78, 80, 89, 98, 99, 100, 132, 140, 144, 148
Chiron .......................................................... 163
Choregos ............................................... 117, 120
Chrestomathia ............................................ 100
Chrysippus .................................................. 148
Cicero ..................................................... 23, 148
Cirrha .......................................................... 138
Classical .................. 16, 25, 34, 166, 167, 169
Clothes ........................................................ 100
Clouds .................................................... 58, 145
Clymena ........................................................ 38
Coeus ...................................................... 15, 146
Coins ................. 19, 39, 108, 109, 110, 115

Colaenis .................................................. 69
Constellation ..................... 60, 63, 104, 155
Contest Of Homer And Hesiod ........... 133
Cordax ...................................... 77, 119
Corfu ........................................ 114, 115
Corinthos ............................. 43, 48, 124
Cratinus ............................................. 141
Cratylus ............................................. 17
Crescent .................... 109, 115, 132, 133
Crete 28, 40, 41, 42, 49, 82, 99, 120, 142, 152
Crown ........................................ 19, 35
Cyclades Islands ................................ 49
Cyclops ............................................. 20
Cynegeticus ............................. 102, 103
Cynergetica ...................................... 116
Cynthia ............................................. 86
Cypress ................................ 71, 162, 163
Cyprus ............................................. 108
Damophyle ....................................... 80
Dance 12, 47, 68, 74, 77, 102, 105, 117, 119, 120, 121, 127, 129, 139
Daphnaií ..................................... 51, 69
De Natura Deorum ......................... 23, 148
Deer 17, 20, 51, 52, 53, 54, 56, 59, 66, 70, 75, 85, 87, 100, 101, 102, 103, 104, 105, 108, 109, 110, 133, 134, 145, 146, 162
Deipnosophistai ............................ 54, 135
Delia .................................................. 86
Delos 25, 28, 29, 32, 49, 50, 57, 62, 65, 78, 86, 106, 129, 143, 157, 163, 164
Delphi .. 26, 48, 57, 117, 130, 135, 137, 146
Delphic Oracle ..................... 36, 90, 130
Delphinion ....................................... 53
Demestrios ........................................ 64
Demeter .... 15, 16, 25, 30, 77, 140, 154, 159
Demetrios ....................................... 147
Demetrius ......................................... 38
Dereatis ............................................ 69
Dereion ...................................... 48, 69
Despoine ......................................... 115
Diamastigosis ................................. 160
Diana 6, 7, 11, 16, 18, 20, 26, 30, 42, 63, 86, 96, 97, 118, 132, 142, 158, 163
Diktaion ......................................... 142
Diktynna 42, 51, 65, 86, 87, 111, 125, 141, 142, 144, 152
Diodorus Siculus 57, 61, 109, 112, 139, 142, 148
Dione ............................................. 118
Dionysiaca 21, 24, 25, 58, 60, 62, 100, 102, 109, 128, 132, 139, 140, 142, 145, 147, 152, 153, 154, 156, 157, 163
Dionysus 16, 56, 57, 58, 86, 100, 109, 110, 113, 114, 118, 131, 140, 141, 142, 143, 150, 152, 154, 155
Disease ................. 61, 67, 74, 131, 133, 161
Dithyrambs: Heracles The Bold ........... 143
Dogs 11, 13, 17, 20, 82, 87, 104, 110, 111, 144, 147, 153, 155, 162
Dragon ..................................... 26, 130
Eagle ........................................ 59, 113

Earth Goddess ............................. 35, 159
Eel ...................................... 112, 123, 150
Egypt .................................. 17, 42, 141
Eileithyia ........................ 31, 69, 70, 99
Eileithyiai ........................... 70, 99, 100
Ekhinos .......................................... 164
Elaphebolia ............................. 51, 52, 53
Elaphebolos ........................ 50, 52, 110
Elaphia ............................................. 51
Elaphiaia ............................. 70, 101, 110
Elaphobolos .................................... 109
Elaphos Cakes ................................. 52
Eleusis .............................................. 48
Eleutherna ....................................... 99
Elis ........................... 48, 66, 80, 101
Emperor Augustus ............................ 78
England ............................................. 4
Enodia .............................................. 70
Enyo ................................................. 85
Eos ................................................. 155
Ephesia ..................... 33, 34, 43, 70, 82
Ephesiaca ....................................... 120
Ephesus 11, 15, 17, 19, 22, 31, 34, 35, 37, 38, 39, 42, 42, 60, 61, 70, 78, 79, 91, 97, 108, 112, 113, 119, 121, 125, 129, 136, 138, 158, 159, 164, 166, 168
Ephialtes .................. 56, See Aloadai Giants
Epidauros ......................................... 48
Eriboia ............................................. 56
Eros ............................. 92, 94, 154
Etymologicum Magnum ................. 23, 38
Euboia ............................ 66, 76, 81, 125
Eukleia ....................................... 70, 71
Eurasinos .......................................... 44
Euripides 21, 43, 78, 79, 95, 100, 118, 120, 136, 143, 158, 161, 164
Eurynomi ......................................... 71
Eustephanos Keladeine ..................... 71
Fabulae ................... 34, 106, 128, 138, 155
Falcon ............................................ 115
Fall Of Troy ..................................... 24
Fasti ....................... 62, 86, 89, 153
Feast Of The Plough ........................ 118
Feet .................................................. 27
Festivals .......................... 43, 50, 51, 76
Fish ................... 36, 71, 108, 111, 112
Frogs ........................... 23, 86, 144
Furies ............................................... 58
Gaia ........................ 15, 62, 63, 88, 90, 135
Gaius ......................................... 38, 167
Galaxion ........................................... 50
Gamelion .......................................... 50
Gaul ............................. 17, 43, 49, 115
Geese ................................................ 17
General Mardonios ............................ 84
Goat ....................... 47, 52, 125, 159
Gold ............ 18, 21, 74, 110, 115, 133, 162
Golden Chariot ..................... 75, 134, 162
Golden Hinds ................................. 110
Golden Wolf ................................... 116
Goldfinch ....................................... 106
Gorgo ..................................... 114, 115

Goths ................................................. 37
Graces ............................................... 117
Great Mother ..................... 18, 22, 42, 159
Greece 17, 42, 43, 46, 48, 49, 66, 71, 72, 76, 77, 87, 101, 111, 124, 151, 155, 157, 158, 164, 166, 167, 168, 170
Greek Magical Papyri ............ 105, 119, 143
Guide To Greece ................................ 24, 33
Guinea-Fowl .................................... 106
Gymnasium ...................................... 44
Hades ................. 15, 62, 77, 122, 131, 139
Hagní Parthenos ............................... 92
Hail .......................................... 58, 145
Hannahanna ..................................... 34
Hare .................................. 59, 104, 113
Hattic .............................................. 35
Healing ................ 11, 27, 82, 96, 119, 158
Hecatean Ides ................................... 97
Hecuba ........................................... 120
Hekaerge ............................ 57, 87, 157
Hekate 11, 15, 16, 28, 31, 34, 40, 46, 54, 57, 59, 60, 65, 66, 67, 69, 70, 73, 81, 84, 85, 87, 88, 90, 94, 96, 99, 100, 111, 118, 124, 134, 135, 143, 144, 154, 159, 164, 168, 169
Hekatebolon Iokheaira ..................... 73, 88
Hekatombaion .................................. 50
Hekatonnesoi Islands ........................ 49
Heleia ............................................. 71
Helen ........................................ 58, 121
Helios ............. 57, 118, 119, 132, 134, 148
Hellenistic ........................ 16, 22, 27, 99
Helos ......................................... 48, 71
Hemere ........................................... 71
Henetoi ....................................... 49, 66
Hephaestus ................................... 145
Hera 15, 25, 26, 28, 31, 32, 46, 47, 56, 58, 60, 69, 70, 71, 88, 98, 99, 109, 130, 142, 144, 145, 147, 148, 168
Herakles ........................ 70, 110, 145, 146
Herbs .............................................. 162
Hermes ....... 56, 69, 106, 129, 139, 141, 155
Hermione ..................................... 48, 73
Herodas ........................................... 27
Herodotus 23, 36, 52, 53, 57, 68, 74, 80, 108, 121, 134, 140, 141
Herostratus ..................................... 37
Hesiod 15, 23, 25, 46, 59, 60, 73, 98, 99, 133, 144, 166, 168
Hestia ..................................... 94, 136
Hestiaia ........................................... 81
Hesychius ................................... 51, 119
Heurippa ......................................... 87
Hiereia ............................................ 72
Hieros ............................................ 50
Hígemoní ................................... 72, 125
Hiketeria .................................... 51, 53
Hippo ...................................... 121, 129
Hippolytus ... 21, 95, 96, 103, 136, 158, 160
Hippomenes ................................... 151
Hipponax ....................................... 141
Histories ......................................... 23
Hittite ............................................ 35

Homer 14, 16, 21, 23, 61, 62, 70, 94, 99, 133, 134, 146, 168, 169
Homeric Hymn 2 To Demeter ..... 122, 139
Homeric Hymn 27 To Artemis 87, 88, 89, 91, 102, 117, 133, 134, 153
Homeric Hymn 3 To Apollo .......... 73, 117
Homeric Hymn 5 To Aphrodite 94, 101, 117, 121
Homeric Hymns .... 23, 25, 31, 74, 111, 117
Honey ................................. 41, 42, 52
Horse ............................. 87, 121, 129
Horus ........................................... 140
Hunters .................... 103, 108, 109, 151
Hunting Spears .............................. 20, 141
Huntress 7, 12, 13, 15, 20, 22, 52, 65, 87, 91, 94, 96, 101, 105, 114, 117, 121, 127, 144
Hyampolis .................................. 48, 52
Hyginus ....... 24, 34, 63, 106, 128, 138, 155
Hyllos ............................................ 65
Hymn 3 To Artemis 61, 71, 77, 80, 87, 88, 89, 90, 91, 99, 101, 102, 110, 119, 120, 121, 124, 126, 127, 129, 133, 134, 135, 137, 142, 146, 148, 149, 150, 151, 152, 153, 155
Hymn 4 To Delos ..................... 29, 87, 157
Hymn Singing Contests .................... 55
Hymnia ...................................... 51, 72
Hyperboreoi ............................... 57, 138
Hypoplakinan Thebes ....................... 49
Hypsous ........................ 48, 51, 69, 87
Iberia ............................................. 49
Iberians .......................................... 43
Ikaria ............................................. 49
Iliad 16, 21, 23, 56, 61, 62, 65, 70, 71, 74, 75, 88, 90, 99, 103, 113, 120, 131, 133, 134, 135, 145, 147, 148, 168
Inatos ............................................. 99
Indian Wars Of Dionysus 58, 125, 142, 145
Iokheaira ................. 73, 88, 101, 117
Ionian League ................................. 34
Iphigeneia 43, 44, 45, 46, 58, 59, 60, 73, 75, 79, 85, 89, 100, 109, 110, 113, 118, 144, 153, 161, 164, 167, 168
Iris ........................................... 31, 32
Isis ........................................... 16, 140
Issoria ...................................... 73, 125
*Issorion* ........................................ 73
Istrus ............................................. 63
Italy ............. 49, 66, 96, 113, 114, 154, 158
Ivory ............................................. 100
Javelin ............................. 66, 120, 155
Jove .............................................. 63
Kalkhas .......................................... 59
Kalliste .......................................... 74
Kallisto ................................ See Callisto
Kalydna .......................................... 49
Kaphya ................................ 48, 67, 76
Kappadokia ..................................... 85
Karya ........................................... 143
Karyae ......................................... 121
Karyai ..................... 48, 67, 74, 117
Karyatis ........................... 74, 117, 143

Kastabos .................................. 49, 158
Kedreatis .......................................... 74
Keladeine ........................ 71, 88, 120
Kephalos ......................................... 155
Keres ............................................... 127
Khersonesos ..................................... 49
Khitone ...................................... 88, 101
Khloris .............................................. 61
Khronios ................................... 72, 128
Khrysaoros ....................................... 74
Khryselakatos ............... 74, 101, 120
Khrysenios ............................... 75, 131
Khrysothronos ................................. 75
Kilikia ............................................... 83
Kindyas ............................................. 75
Kindye ............................................... 75
King Croesus, Also See Croesus ............. 36
King Dion ....................................... 143
King Kodors .................................... 36
King Lygdamis ................................ 60
King Minos, Also See Minos ........ 142, 152
King Oineus ......................... 106, 108
King Tantalus .................................. 61
King Xerxes ..................................... 43
Kingtantalos .................................. 102
Kirrha ............................................... 48
Kite ................................................. 116
Kithaironian Lion ........................... 65
Kleanthes ......................................... 66
Knageus ............................................ 75
Knagia ...................................... 75, 125
Knakalísia ......................................... 75
Knakeatis .......................................... 75
Kokkoka ............................................ 76
Kolainis ............................................. 76
Koloínís ............................................ 76
Komana ............................................ 85
Kondyleatis ...................................... 76
Korakios ........................................... 49
Kordax ............................ 77, See Cordax
Kore .................................................. 77
Korone ........................................ 48, 89
Koronis ........................................... 129
Koryphaia ......................................... 77
Korythaleia ...................................... 77
Korythalia ................... 51, 77, 119, 125
Kos ................................... 27, 75, 129
Kouretes ......................................... 108
Kourotrophos ............. 77, 88, 98, 99
Krateriskoi ....................................... 44
Krokotoi ........................................... 46
Kronos ..................... 15, 41, 67, 68, 99
Kybele ...... 16, 34, 64, 66, 85, 151, 154, 159
Kynosoura ....................................... 74
Kynosourian Bitches .................... 110
Kyrene ........................................... 153
Kyrtones .......................................... 48
Labruanda ............................ 40, 41, 42
Lacedaemon 51, 69, 73, 74, 84, 87, 117, 121, 125, 143
Lactantius ........................... 24, 42, 67
Ladomeia ....................................... 131
Lady Of The Beasts ........................ 18
Laertes ........................................... 150
Lagina ........................................ 40, 99
Lake Gygaia .............................. 49, 76
Lake Koloe ...................................... 76
Lakedaimonion Politeia ........... 23, 161
Laphria ................................. 51, 53, 78
Laphros ............................................ 78
Lato .................................................. 99
Latona ........................... 63, 106, See Leo
Laurel ......................... 51, 69, 77. 162
Leimon ........................................... 129
Lenaion ............................................ 50
Leopard ..................... 17, 18, 113, 114
Leros ................................................ 89
Lesbos .............................................. 65
Leto 15, 16, 25, 26, 27, 28, 31, 32, 56, 61, 62, 63, 76, 80, 88, 90, 91, 95, 98, 99, 106, 114, 116, 117, 127, 129, 130, 131, 135, 137, 138, 142, 143, 144, 145, 146, 147, 163
Letrinoi ..................................... 48, 66
Leukophruíní ................................. 78
Life Of Apollonius Of Tyana ..... 24, 80, 84
Life Of Theseus ............................. 53
Lilaia ................................................ 48
Limenoskope .................................. 88
Limnai ....................................... 48, 78
Limnaia .................................. 111, 123
Limnaion ......................................... 45
Lion .......... 18, 70, 104, 113, 114, 115, 151, 153
Lítois ................................................ 88
Lives ........................................ 73, 126
Lokhia ..................................... 78, 164
Lomaitho ................................ 86, 130
Lousa ............................................... 72
Lousoi ..................................... 48, 163
Loxo ....................................... 57, 157
Lucina .............................................. 31
Lustration ....................................... 47
Lycaon ............................................. 60
Lydia ................... 76, 77, 81, 115, 119
Lygodesmí ....................................... 89
Lykeíí ....................................... 79, 115
Lykoa ........................................ 48, 79
Lyre ......................................... 20, 117
Lysistrata ................................... 46, 89
Lysizonos Gune .............................. 47
Ma .......................................... 85, 105
Macedonia ....................................... 37
Magna Mater ............. 22, 34, 42, 159
Magnesia ................................... 49, 78
Maia ....................................... 60, 155
Maimakterion .................................. 50
Makaria-Eukleia ............................ 158
Marathon ........................................ 52
Marios .............................................. 48
Massilia ...................... 43, 49, 115
Mastic ............................................ 142
Medea .............................................. 57
Megalopolis ...................... 43, 48, 83
Megara .................................. 48, 65, 84

Melanippos .................................. 86, 130
Meleagrides .................................. 106
Meleagros .................................... 151
Meliboia ........................... See Khloris
Melissa ............................... 19. 41, 42
Melite ........................................ 49, 157
Meliteus ........................................ 41
Mēn ......................................... 66, 85
Mesopotamia .................................. 17
Messene ...................................... 48, 90
Messenia ........................................ 89
Metageitnion ............................... 50, 67
Metamorphoses 20, 21, 23, 24, 58, 59, 86, 88, 89, 104, 108, 128, 133, 141, 150, 151, 152, 155
Meteor .......................................... 41
Miletos ......................................... 49
Minoan Lady Of The Beasts ................. 90
Minos ................................. 40, 65, 87
Minotaur ................................... 84, 109
Moon 1, 3, 4, 7, 9, 11, 12, 54, 85, 90, 97, 99, 110, 132, 133, 135, 148, 162, 168
Moralia ......................................... 77
Mother Of The Gods ...................... 15, 159
Mothone ........................................ 48
Mount Artemisios ............................. 48
*Mount Cynthus* ............................... 86
Mount Knakalos ............................... 75
Mount Koryphon ........................... 48, 77
Mount Krathis ............................. 48, 82
Mount Lykone ............................. 48, 80
Mount Mainalos ............................... 79
Mount Ossa ..................................... 56
Mount Sipylos ............................. 49, 62
Mountains ...... 13, 15, 65, 94, 101, 102, 148
Mounykhia ............ 48, 50, 51, 54, 79, 104
Mounykhion ......................... 53, 54, 79
Mugwort ...................................... 163
Muses .................................... 117, 153
Mycenaean ...................... 16, 34, 90, 169
Myrrhinos ................................. 48, 83
Myrtle ................................. 113, 142, 162
Myrto ........................................... 70
Mysia ........................................... 79
Natio ........................................... 31
Natural History ................................ 23
Naupaktos .................................. 48, 66
Nausicaa ...................................... 120
Naxos ..................................... 57, 158
Necklace ............................. 18, 19, 39
Nemesis ........................... 18, 62, 140, 147
Nemi .................................. 96, 97, 158
Nemoralia ...................................... 97
Nemydia ....................................... 80
Neolithic ................................... 34, 44
Nikaia .................................. 143, 154
Nike ............................................ 18
Niobe ......... 61, 62, 102, 127, 130, 137, 146
Nonnus ................................ 21, 24, 157
Nymph 87, 96, 118, 123, 124, 128, 143, 150, 153, 154, 155

Nymphs 20, 21, 62, 74, 95, 98, 112, 118, 119, 120, 143, 147, 148, 149, 157
Oak ....................................... 76, 163
Oceanides ................................. 98, 149
Odes .......................................... 155
Odysseus .................................. 87, 150
Odyssey 16, 21, 73, 75, 90, 101, 120, 131, 134, 135, 143, 147, 150, 167
Oedipus The King ........................ 21, 135
Oiantheia ...................................... 48
Old Physics .................................. 148
Olen Of Lycia ................................. 29
Olive ........................................... 53
Olympia .................... 15, 48, 51, 64, 69, 70
Olympian .................. 15, 25, 56, 141, 145
Olympias ....................................... 36
Olympic Games .............................. 164
Olympus ............... 31, 125, 135, 137, 146
On Animals 24, 82, 105, 106, 112, 120, 123, 150
Opis ........................................ 57, 62
Oppian ................................. 115, 116
Oracle 36, 44, 83, 84, 104, 108, 112, 113, 118, 134, 140, 161, 164
Oracle Of Delphi, Also See Delphi ....... 15
Orestes ........................... 44, 59, 75, 85
Oresthasion ............................... 48, 72
Orion ............... 57, 62, 63, 102, 129, 155
Orkhomenos ........................ 48, 51, 72, 74
Orneai .......................................... 48
Orphic Hymn 2 To Prothyraia ......... 69, 70
Orphic Hymn 36 To Artemis .86, 101, 142
Orphic Hymns ....................... 23, 101, 142
Orsilokhia ................................. 89, 99
Orthia ........ 45, 80, 100, 114, 121, 125, 160
Orthosia ....................................... 80
Ortygia 7, 27, 28, 30, 31, 32, 49, 89, 106, 112, 123, 129, 133, 150
Osiris ......................................... 140
Otos ..................... 56, See Aloadai Giants
Otrera ........................................ 138
Oupis ..................................... 57, 157
Ouranos ................................. 15, 135
Ovid 21, 23, 25, 59, 62, 86, 88, 89, 108, 128, 133, 141, 150, 151, 153, 155
Ozolian Lokris ................................ 66
Paean ......................................... 118
Pagai ...................................... 48, 84
Paidotrophos ............................. 89, 98
Palm ...................................... 79, 163
Pamphylia ..................................... 80
Pan .......................... 110, 123, 147, 154, 155
Panemos ....................................... 50
Parthenon ..................................... 44
Parthenon Aidoine ........................... 89
Parthenos .......................... 89, 92, 93, 158
Partridge ................................ 104, 105
Patrai ................... 48, 53, 78, 86, 110, 130
Pausanias 24, 25, 26, 33, 34, 43, 44, 45, 46, 51, 53, 60, 61, 62, 64, 65, 66, 67, 68, 69, 70, 71, 72, 73, 74, 75, 76, 77, 78, 79, 80, 81, 82, 83, 84, 85, 86, 87, 89, 90, 95, 98, 101, 103,

109, 110, 113, 115, 117, 119, 121, 122, 123, 124, 125, 128, 129, 130, 136, 142, 144, 146, 147, 150, 157, 158, 161
Peace .................................................. 46
Peirene ............................................. 124
Peirithous ........................................ 121
Peisistratos ....................................... 44
Peitho ............................................... 80
Pelias ................................................ 57
Pellene .............................................. 48
Peloponnese ............................... 43, 101
Pergaia .............................................. 80
Perge ........................................... 49, 80
Persephone ....................... 122, 139, 148
Perses ................................................ 28
Perseus ...................................... 58, 170
Persia ................................................ 81
Persian ............. 34, 43, 45, 52, 134, 158
Phelloi .............................................. 48
Pheneos ...................................... 48, 87
Pherai .................................. 49, 70, 81
Phigalia ................................ 48, 71, 84
Philip II ........................................... 37
Phintias .......................................... 108
Phlya ................................................ 48
Phocis ......................................... 52, 82
Phoebe ........ 15, 89, 90, 134, 135, 137, 146
Phoebus ............... 89, 92, 117, 135, 138
Phoibaian Lagoon ........................ 82, 103
Pholoe ..................................... 123, 154
Phosphorus ...................................... 90
Phrygia ............................................. 49
Phyla ................................................ 83
Phylomone ..................................... 154
Phylonoe ........................................ 158
Pindar ............ 23, 25, 129, 142, 143, 155
Pine ................................................ 142
Piraeus ............................................. 54
Pisa .................................................. 48
Pitane ............................................... 49
Plague ......................................... 47, 61
Plataia .............................................. 48
Plato ................................... 17, 23, 141
Pleiades .................................... 118, 155
Pleione ........................................... 155
Plutarch 24, 37, 53, 67, 70, 71, 73, 77, 81, 121, 126, 132, 154, 158
Polyboia ........................... See Phylonoe
Polyphonte ....................... 103, 104, 136
*Pomegranate* .................................... 76
Poppies ........................................... 163
Poppy ............................................. 163
Poseidon ................. 15, 27, 50, 145, 152
Potamoi ........................................... 98
Potna Thea ....................................... 90
Potnia .......... 7, 17, 18, 19, 40, 90, 103, 107
*Potnia Theron* ........ 7, 17, 18, 19, 40, 90, 103
Pregnancy ............... 25, 60, 129, 130
Pregnant ................... 60, 100, 116, 146
Proclus ........................................... 100
Proitos ........................................ 72, 77
Prokris ........................................... 155

Prometheus .................................... 146
Propylaii .......................................... 81
Proseoia ........................................... 81
Prostitution ..................................... 97
Prothyraia ........................................ 70
Protothronií ..................................... 82
Proverbia Aesopi ............................ 119
Pseudo-Hyginus ............................... 27
Purification .................................... 130
Pyanopsion ...................................... 50
Pygela ........................................ 49, 79
Pylai .......................................... 49, 83
Pyronia ............................................ 82
Pyrrhikhos ................... 48, 68, 121, 125
Pyrrichists ........................ 120, 126, 139
Pythian .......................................... 129
Python ............. 26, 27, 90, 130, 137, 146
Quail ........................... 28, 32, 104, 106
Quintus Smyrnaeus ................... 24, 114
Renoir ............................................. 20
Rex Nemorensus .............................. 96
Rhea ............... 15, 16, 28, 64, 68, 99, 159
Rhodes .................................. 15, 18, 49
Rhokkha .......................................... 82
Roman 7, 16, 17, 18, 19, 20, 22, 30, 31, 35, 42, 45, 58, 62, 86, 97, 99, 115, 132, 136, 154, 160, 168, 169
Roman Catholic Church ................... 94
Sabazios ......................................... 141
Sacred Springs ........................ 111, 123
Saffron ...................................... 46, 104
Sailors ............................................. 28
Salamis ....................................... 48, 54
Salt ............................................ 33, 38
Samos ........................................ 49, 52
Sappho ............................................ 94
Sardis .............................................. 76
Saron ......................................... 51, 82
Saron Of Troizenos ........................ 103
Saronia ....................................... 51, 82
Saronis ............................................ 82
Sarpedonia ...................................... 83
Scapegoats ....................................... 55
Scorpio ...................................... 62, 63
Scourging .................................. 84, 161
Scythia ................................ 49, 60, 84
Scythians ......................................... 44
Sea ..................................... 27, 28, 32
Sea Of Pontos .................................. 59
Sekhmet ......................................... 131
Selasphoros ..................................... 83
Selcuk .................................. 28, 35, 39
Selene ... 11, 16, 96, 132, 134, 143, 148, 168
Selinus ............................................. 36
Serpent ..................... 26, 115, 130, 144
Servius .......................................... 143
Sesame ............................................ 52
Seven Wonders Of The Ancient World 11, 15, 34
Shapeshifting ..................... 28, 56, 145
She-Bear ............. 46, 47, 104, 119, 151
Sheela-Na-Gig ............................... 114

Sicily ............... 17, 49, 112, 123, 139, 150
Sikyon ................................................. 48, 147
Silvae ........................ 123, 147, 149, 154
Silver ....................................... 133, 162
Skephros ........................................... 129
Skias ............................................. 48, 83
Skiatis ................................................. 83
Skillos ................................................. 48
Skirophorion ...................................... 50
Sky God ...................................... 35, 159
Skythia ............................... 84, 85, 109
Skythoi ............................................. 84
Snood ............................................... 21
Song .................................................. 27
Soothsayer ................................. 59, 100
Sophocles ..................... 21, 119, 135
Soteira ..................... 84, 109, 123, 150
Sow ................................................ 108
Sparta 33, 48, 51, 65, 72, 73, 79, 114, 118, 120, 121, 125, 160
Spear ........................... 20, 56, 120, 162
Spring ........................... 45, 123, 150
St John ............................................. 34
St Paul .............................................. 38
St. George ......................................... 44
Stag 18, 20, 52, 101, 109, 110, 114, 128, 149, 152
Stars ........................... 60, 62, 63, 105, 155
Stater ............................................... 22
Statius .............................................. 23
Statius Thebaid ............................... 67
Strabo 17, 23, 25, 36, 43, 66, 68, 69, 70, 71, 75, 76, 78, 79, 80, 83, 85, 103, 125, 131, 138, 148, 158, 163, 170
Stymphalia ............................... 85, 145
Stymphalian Birds ................... 85, 145
Stymphalian Nymphs ...................... 85
Stymphalos ..................... 48, 85, 145
Suicide ...................... 61, 67, 72, 140
Suidas ............ 24, 47, 64, 79, 104, 105, 147
Suppliants ................................ 79, 144
Swan ...................... 17, 106, 107, 114
Sword ........................ 120, 139, 161, 162
Syracuse ............ 28, 30, 49, 112, 123, 150
Syria .......................................... 17, 71
Syrinx ...................... 96, 133, 136, 155
Taboo ............................................. 103
Tanagra ........................................... 48
Taureans ................................... 45, 59
Tauria .............................................. 85
Tauris ................................... 43, 44, 166
Tauropolos ........................ 44, 85, 109
Tauros ................................ 59, 85, 153
Taygete .......................................... 148
Tegea ........................ 48, 72, 76, 128
Tellus .............................................. 63
Teuthia ........................................... 80
Teuthis ........................................... 48
Teuthrone ................................... 48, 73
Thargelia ...................... 32, 51, 55, 138
Thargelion ................... 32, 50, 55, 138
The Bible ........................................ 38

The Birds ............................ 69, 76, 106
The Contest Of Homer & Hesiod ......... 23
The Hellenica .................................. 71
The Histories .................................. 53
The Library .............. 23, 56, 128, 151
The Offering Of The Winners .............. 20
The Republic ................................. 141
The Suppliants ............................... 79
The Thracian Women ................. 141
Thebaid Of Statius ......................... 67
Thebes ......... 48, 51, 61, 70, 71, 79, 128
Themistocles ........................... 67, 81
Themistokles ................................. 67
Theocritus ............................. 113, 114
Theognis ....................................... 127
Theroskopos ................... 88, 91, 101
Theseus ......... 57, 84, 109, 121, 143, 160
Thesmophoria ........................ 94, 95
Thesmophoriazusae ................... 101
Thespesion .................................... 84
Thessalia .................... 49, 57, 81, 129
Thestio .......................................... 108
Thrace .......................................... 103
Titan 21, 25, 90, 100, 139, 143, 146, 147, 155, 164
Tityoktone ..................................... 91
Tityos ........................ 91, 131, 134, 137
Torch 31, 54, 58, 115, 121, 126, 135, 142, 144, 162, 164
Torch Races ................................. 164
Triballoi ....................................... 103
Trikka ........................................... 129
Triklaria ......................................... 86
Trikolonoi ...................................... 48
Trioditis ......................................... 97
Trivia ............................................. 96
Troia .............................................. 68
Troizenos ............... 48, 51, 82, 84, 160
Trojan War .......................... 16, 58, 145
Trojan Women .................... 119, 120
Troy ................. 59, 66, 100, 102, 113
Türkiye .......... 16, 17, 28, 40, 49, 85, 99
Twin Serpents ............................. 115
Ursa Major ............................. 60, 104
Valerius Flaccus .......................... 146
Virgil .............................................. 23
Virgin 12, 14, 15, 53, 62, 70, 84, 89, 92, 93, 94, 95, 105, 122, 136, 139, 143, 155, 158
Virgin Births .................................. 93
Virginity 12, 47, 60, 67, 92, 93, 94, 95, 96, 97, 140, 147, 153, 156, 157
Walnut ................................... 74, 163
Warrior .......................................... 95
Water ............. 20, 27, 47, 123, 128, 132
Wolf ......... 26, 54, 66, 103, 109, 115, 116
Wool .............................................. 53
Wormwood ................................. 163
Wrestling ....................................... 44
Xenophon 23, 51, 71, 102, 103, 120, 125, 161
Xerxes ........................................... 45
Zalmoxis ...................................... 141

Zeus 15, 16, 20, 25, 26, 27, 28, 32, 37, 40, 41, 42, 56, 58, 60, 61, 63, 71, 73, 90, 94, 99, 101, 106, 109, 114, 115, 118, 124, 134, 139, 142, 143, 144, 145, 146, 147, 148, 149, 152, 155, 164, 167, 168, 169

Zoitea .......................................................... 48
Zoster ................................................... 26, 48

www.ingramcontent.com/pod-product-compliance
Lightning Source LLC
Chambersburg PA
CBHW011948150426
43194CB00017B/2846